SCOTTISH SUPERSTITIONS

Raymond Lamont-Brown

Chambers

Published 1990 by W & R Chambers Ltd,
43-45 Annandale Street, Edinburgh EH7 4AZ

© Raymond Lamont-Brown, 1990

British Library Cataloguing in Publication Data
Lamont-Brown, Raymond
  Scottish superstitions.–(Chambers mini guides series)
  1. Scottish superstitions
  I. Title
  398'.41

  ISBN 0-550-20059-2

Illustrations by John Haxby
Cover design by John Marshall

Typeset by Bookworm Typesetting Ltd, Edinburgh
Printed in Singapore by
Singapore National Printers Ltd

Contents

Preface

WHEN you have washed your windows, or polished the car, do you search the sky for signs of rain clouds? If you do, you are being as superstitious as your ancestors were, for you are enacting a relic of rain-making magic.

Superstitious beliefs involve everyone at some time or another. Today superstition is alive and well in Scotland which has one of the richest funds of superstitious lore in Europe. Perhaps these days we don't believe, as our ancestors did, that to wear a sprig of parsley in the hat would be a cure for headaches, or that warts would be cleared up by crawling through a gorse bush backwards. But many still take care not to walk under a ladder, kick a cat, whistle in a theatre and some people do not fail to throw a pinch of spilled salt over the shoulder just in case.

Superstition is not just avoiding the colour green for a dress, or carrying a favourite mascot in the pocket, it is a living force that is triggered off when a person is afraid, or is anxious about a situation that is beyond his or her control. Superstition is derived from the Latin words *super* (above) and *stare* (to stand) – those who survived battle in ancient times were called *superstites* because they outlived their comrades – and they remain as relics of long dead cultures and forgotten ways of life. But superstitions are as fresh and modern as the latest invention. So this book is a voyage of exploration into Scotland's hidden traditions and secret culture. It covers the whole gamut of Scots life from colours and numbers to birds, animals and flowers, and from the superstitions of trade and industry to the beliefs of childhood and old age.

Where possible the origins of Scotland's superstitions are traced, but sometimes they defy modern explanation, for the circumstances that gave them life are long forgotten. Yet, in the Borders they still remember how rowan twigs keep witches away, and at Craigievar they still point out the footprint left by the Devil whose presence is summoned up when you . . . read the book and find out!

Creatures of the Sea and River

STAND by any of Scotland's sea lochs and watch the **seals** at play. As they splash and dive, it is easy to imagine how the Celtic legends of seal-people were evolved about these delightful sea creatures who were deemed able to slough their skins at will and take on the likeness of humans.

The grey seals who crowd the rocky skerries of the northern isles were called the Selkie Folk, who would assume this human form on Midsummer Eve to dance on the shore without their furs. The old superstitions about them were specific. If a mortal found a seal skin soon after the period of transformation from seal to human, they would have power over that seal-person.

The folk around Loch Duich, in Ross and Cromarty, still tell the sad story of the three brothers who, one night, watched a group of seals come ashore, doff their pelts and gambol on the moonlit beach. The brothers were particularly taken by three seal-maidens and stole their skins. So when the seal-people returned to the water's edge, the three maidens were forced to stay behind. Seeing the distress of one of the seal-maidens the youngest brother gave back her skin and she slipped gracefully beneath the waves. His two brothers kept the other seal-maidens and married them.

A few nights later, the seal-people returned and the two brothers locked their wives away in case they were called back. The youngest brother watched the seal-people dance on the beach and mourned for the loss of his own seal-love.

Then, the story goes, the seal leader, father of the seal-maiden the youngest brother had loved, gave permission for him to marry his daughter and they lived a life of complete happiness on shore. But the other two brothers only knew unhappiness. One seal-wife found her skin and returned to the depths; and warned by this the eldest brother burned his wife's skin to stop her from going back. Alas, in a terrible house fire which followed the skin burning the seal-wife perished.

Seal-men were also believed to come on land to marry mortal women. The offspring of such unions were said to have webbed toes and fingers, or scales on the soles of their feet. Certain clans in Scotland were thought to be descendants of the seal-folk. Several of the Mackays of Sutherland were known as 'the descendants of the seal', particularly the family of the lairds of Borgie. The same was said of the MacCodruns of North Uist and the McPhees of Colonsay.

Another sea-folk who were said to dwell with humans were the Fin-Men and Fin-Wives whose offspring were the **mermaids** and **mermen** who were all bent on securing human spouses. Mermaids would lure young men to their city of Finfolkaheem, beneath the sea. The old folk told of the summer home of the Fin-folk at Eynhallow, Orkney's sacred isle which was said to vanish at certain times. Fin-folk could only be got rid of by throwing a silver coin into the sea.

In the realm of the Mither o' the Sea – the sea deity of Scottish waters invoked by fishermen for protection against the Devil and Teran, lord of sea-storms – was many a sea monster. The most common was the **Stoor Worm**, a serpent-like creature that attacked boats. Then there was the *brigdi*, a huge flat creature with fins to pull boats down, the *seefer*, a kind of whale, and the *sefin*, which was like descriptions of the Loch Ness Monster, in that it had a series of humps and a long neck.

All of these sea-creatures must be regularly petitioned for good luck by offerings of food and flowers thrown into the sea, the old superstitions said. In the days of Celtic heathendom this was the job of one of the female shamans of the tribe who expiated the tribe's accumulated sins by casting the offerings into the waves with incantations and ritual gestures. A folkloric relic of this is enacted each July at the Berwickshire fishing town of Eyemouth within the Festival of the Herring Queen. The festival was instituted in 1939 and grew out of the old 'fishermen's picnic', itself decades old. The queen-elect comes into Eyemouth harbour on a local boat and is landed at Gunsgreen where she is crowned and personifies the town's 'luck' for a full year.

Fishermen are perhaps the most superstitious people on earth and they add a colourful range of superstitions to the lore of Scotland's creatures of sea and shore. Many believed, for instance, that **seagulls** were really the souls of dead seamen given new life, particularly those who had been drowned at sea. Thus it was thought unlucky to kill a seagull. Should a seagull fly against the window of a house it was deemed a warning of danger to some member of the family who dwelt therein but who was away at sea. Three gulls flying together was always a death omen for seafarers.

The idea that **barnacle geese** were actually hatched from rotting ships' timbers, was a common old wives' tale in medieval Scotland. The superstition lived on in the more modern concept that barnacles on a ship's bottom would turn into geese.

Scots seamen have long regarded **porpoises** as fortune-bringing creatures, which should never be harmed. Some said they kept sharks away, and to see a group of them playing near a ship was a good sign for the trip as they would lead the ship to good catches or a safe port; but their more boisterous gambols foretold a gale to come.

3

Eels come in for some superstitious thought too, and many a fisherman wore the skin of an eel around his upper leg to prevent cramp in cold conditions. Along the Scottish Border though, any river pool that contained a lamprey (or ramper-eel) was avoided by swimmers lest the creature seized hold and drew blood.

Fish were always thought to have supernatural knowledge and wisdom, and were particularly upset by violent happenings in the water. Should blood be spilled in the sea, the old fishermen said, the white fish shoals would disappear for years. The folklorist Eleanor Hull came across the story of how **herring** were driven away from Loch Carron when two fishermen drowned themselves in these waters off Ross and Cromarty. To expiate the 'bad luck' which had ensued the local fishermen built two huge bonfires at the place where the men's bodies were found, to appease the fish.

To catch a **carp** meant a full purse for a year, while a live eel in a man's drink was a sure cure for drunkenness. Also, the **tench** was long known by Scottish fishermen as the 'physician of the waters' for its supposed healing powers. Salt herring rubbed on the feet would cure a sore throat, it was believed, and **skate** could be lured into a net with fiddle music.

A catch should never be counted as this would inhibit future success, but should the first single catch of the season be a female fish the year's hauls would be good. This superstition was also applied to shore and loch anglers. A shoal of fish could be turned away by careless eating some said: a herring, a **pilchard** or a **mackerel** should always be eaten from tail to head, or the fish would turn their heads away from the nets.

From the Isle of Whithorn to St Abbs, the **tide** was always considered a good indication of what was to come. Fisherfolk said that births were more likely to occur on a flowing tide and that death came in the ebb. New nets and lines were best made when the tide was rising. This work was always completed with a libation of whisky for good luck.

Lord Nelson was superstitious enough to order a **horseshoe** to be nailed to the mast of his flagship HMS

Victory for good luck, following the superstition of a thousand years of seamen that iron was a good defence against evil. For, when aboard his ship the sailor was at his most superstitious. It was regarded as very unlucky to lose a **bucket**, or **mop** or **food utensil** overboard, for the items would take the 'ship's luck' away with them.

The fisherman's world was one of **taboos**. It was always regarded as unlucky for a woman who had menfolk at sea to comb her hair after nightfall . . . that's what the mermaids did on the shore to lure young seamen to the depths. And it was very unlucky for a fisherman to see a **rat**, a **cat**, or a **clergyman** before boarding. There was a vigorous taboo language as well. The words **hare**, **fox**, **rabbit** and **pig** were all avoided as they described creatures of evil the old saws (or proverbs) said. The word '**dog**' should not be spoken at sea either, and few would take either a dog or cat aboard a ship; they both brought bad luck, the one luring ships into bad seas and the other, barking on board, brought death. '**Drowning**' was a word never uttered on board, for obvious reasons, but the eschewing of the word '**eggs**' had a more hidden origin. It was a common superstition that eggs were used by witches to transport themselves across water, hence fisher children were taught to break a hole in the bottom of their eggs when they had finished eating them. So other words were used instead of these – 'roundabout' for an egg, 'the mannie wi' the white collar' for a clergyman, and 'the grunter' for a pig.

One should never **whistle** at sea the old salts said for fear of summoning up a wind, and others believed that a wind could be brought to hold in readiness for a calm. As recently as 1814 an old Scotswoman, Maggie Forsythe, who believed in occult power, used to sell little bags of breeze to sea captains to avoid becalming. On one trip to the Isle of Man, Sir Walter Scott bought a knotted string which served the same purpose. The raising of winds was within the province of witches the hoary fishermen said. The witch in Shakespeare's *The Tempest* 'could control the moon, make floods and ebbs', and the Scottish witch Agnes Sampson, in the curious North Berwick Witches case of 1591, was accused of raising a wind to destroy the ship carrying King James VI.

The old folk said that the sea regularly demanded a
toll of lives, and so it was with certain **rivers** which were
judged to require a definite number of lives per year; or
every three years, or every seven. This old idea had its
roots in river worship when the tribesmen believed that
the river was a live creature to be petitioned for good
fortune. So, by river bank and loch side people would
gather to placate the water spirits with gifts of bread,
grain and flowers; a development from the ritual of live
sacrifice.

In some places the most Scottish of water spirits
would appear. The **kelpie**, or water-horse, was feared
all over Scotland. Often it manifested as a mortal horse
which lured the unwary rider to it. Once mounted the
kelpie would gallop off with its rider into the river to
certain drowning.

An unnamed spirit in the River Tweed is thought to
take one life a year. Tweed fishermen would throw a
plaid into the water once a year in the hope that the
spirit would be satisfied with that. Salt, too, was cast
into the waters and over salmon nets to placate the
spirits. The **salmon**, the wisest of all fish for its unerring
sense of direction, had to be so protected. They threw
salt into the Spey as well, and into the Dean Water,
Angus, which was said to claim one life every seven
years. The occult power of the River Till is remembered
in this ominous rhyme:

'Tweed said to Till,
What gars ye rin so still?   *makes you run*
Till said to Tweed,
Though ye rin wi' speed,
And I rin slaw,
For ae man that ye droon
I droon twa.'

Two other Scottish rivers come into rhyming lore:

'Bloodthirsty Dee, each year needs three [*deaths*]
But bonny Don, she needs none.'

Mention of the rivers would not be complete without
including **bridges**, which, because they link one place

with another, have long played an important role in Scottish superstitious belief. When the Romans first bridged Scotland's rivers they brought with them the old belief that as a river was a living thing to cross, it might be an affront to the river gods to proceed without invoking them; so certain sacrifices had to be enacted. Puppets made out of reeds (to represent men, bound hand and foot), called *argei*, were cast into the river on the Ides of May (15th) to placate the river gods. In Scotland the walling-up of a mouse or small bird in the foundations of a new bridge was another superstition used to defy demons and protect those who crossed the bridge.

The building of bridges in Scotland was associated with the Devil, who, it was said, would only allow a bridge to stay up if he was given the soul of the first creature to cross the new bridge. Thus it was considered very unlucky to be the first to cross a new bridge, so a herd of pigs or a flock of sheep was first driven over instead. The key-stone (the stone at the apex of the arch of a bridge) was the most mystic part of the structure and, should you be pursued by demons, you had to race to the bridge and once past the key-stone the old saw said, the demons could not get you. Robert Burns remembered this old superstition when he was writing *Tam O'Shanter* (1790); he had Tam ride hell for leather to the 'key-stane' of Doon Bridge, because, to throw off the witches, water had to be safely crossed: 'A running stream they dare na cross', Burns wrote.

Snow, rain, dew, springs, wells and also rivers were all given presiding deities by the superstitious. **Dew** was the most sacred of the water forms and the liquid was carefully collected in stones hollowed out for the purpose. To bathe, or anoint oneself, with this precious liquid made one able to defy all ill-luck in all its forms, and assured a beautiful countenance for a year. Not for nothing did Scots girls go out on May morning (1st May) in search of the dew.

Folk said a bargain made over running water was unbreakable. 'Water is my witness' was the old saying, and many a Scots farmer stills spits in his hand before striking palms to clinch a bargain – it's the old superstition of calling up water as a testifier.

All over Scotland too were scores of **sacred wells**, wherein water spirits were judged to work magic for good and evil. St John's Well, Balmanno, Kincardine, was visited by parents with their children who had eye trouble or rickets. The waters of Trinity Gash, Perthshire, were thought to protect against plague, and all sores could be cured at the Kirkden Well, Angus, while cures for insanity might be sought of the spirits of the wells of St Fillans, Tyndrum, and St Catherine's, Edinburgh.

Days, Months, Seasons of the Year

SCOTLAND'S superstitions about days mingle for us still with Christian and pagan traditions concerning the timing of events and the need to capture the influence of the planets in their courses. The old folk labelled several days as 'black' (i.e. unlucky) days for Scotland: 'Black Friday' was the day when the news arrived in London that, on 6 December 1745, Prince Charles Edward Stuart had marched into Derby on his way to conquer London and the Hanoverian kingdom, only to march out again with Scotland's Stuart cause no further forward. 'Black Saturday' was the 4 August 1621 when a violent storm occurred at the very moment of the Scottish Parliamentary sitting which forced Episcopalianism on the Scots people.

Here's what Scots believed about the various days of the week:

Sunday, **ruled by the Sun.** A day for finding buried treasure, or seeking support for a venture; for engendering friendship and harmony. Those born on Sunday were deemed secure from the malevolence of evil spirits, and it was once the most favourite day for marriage.

To begin a voyage on a Sunday was thought propitious and many Scottish fishing fleets set off on that day for this reason. To rise from a sick bed on a Sunday meant full recovery, especially if the sick person wore a new garment on that occasion for the first time. To ward off bad luck on a Sunday, nails should never be cut on that day, nor should a bed be turned; if such a thing be done then a sweetheart would be lost.

Monday, **ruled by the Moon.** The spey-wives (wise women) warned not to move house on a Monday lest evil be attracted to your door, but all householders were to expect many dishes broken in the kitchen on this day. In certain parts of the Borders it was judged unlucky to meet a flat-footed person on a

Monday, especially if you were starting a journey. Some butchers would not kill pigs on Mondays lest the meat shrink and be of less value. Yet it was a day on which to see visions and conduct important matters to do with love.

***Tuesday*, ruled by Mars, God of War.** The day of discord, when the spirits of the dead might be summoned to do mortal will, Tuesday was not the time to meet a left-handed person first thing in the morning. Maybe this was a race memory of the Danes who once raided Scottish shores, for their god Tiw, some said, gave his name to this day. Tiw was left-handed and sacrificed his left hand to rid the world of the power of Fenris-Wolf.

***Wednesday*, ruled by Mercury.** Not a good day to begin a journey, the old folk said, but 'the best day of all' for a wedding. If you sneezed on a Wednesday you were deemed to be going to be in receipt of an important letter. And Wednesday was the day to increase knowledge, divine the future and conduct good trade.

***Thursday*, ruled by Jupiter.** The day when you could look for gains in money, status and friendship, Thursday was also a favoured day to carry out a difficult task.

***Friday*, ruled by Venus.** The old texts say this is a day for 'love, lust and pleasure', and few Scots had much good to say about the day because it was reckoned to be the day of the Crucifixion. 'Friday sail, always fail' the old fishermen recounted, mirroring the old superstition that it was bad luck to move house on a Friday as well as a Monday. But, contradicting the above view that Friday is for love, it was also thought ill advised to go courting on a Friday — Adam and Eve were driven out of the Garden of Eden on that day! Good Friday had several superstitions concerned with it varying in different parts of Scotland. By and large it was considered a day of rest, particularly for blacksmiths, carpenters and all who worked with iron tools. Bread baked on this day would have curative properties and those born on Good Friday would be given the Second Sight and would be neither hanged nor drowned. As a lucky charm you should preserve an egg on this day, and decorate the house with branches of rowan.

Saturday, **ruled by Saturn.** Believed by some to be the best day for Baptism, to bring good luck to the child, Saturday was considered another day of ill omen in certain parts of Scotland. A day long associated with death, destruction and injury Saturday, noted a country tradition, was a good day for planting out seedlings.

Specific days like New Year's Day, Candlemas Day (2 February: Christmas decorations must be taken down on this day, or the devil would enter a house and do it himself), and Hallowe'en (31 October) all had individual superstitions connected with the customs of the day, as did the months and seasons of the year.

In Scotland, of course, the days of the week were all associated with the dread names of the Gods of the Nordic pantheon: Sunday and Monday were mild enough, being names respectively after the sun and moon, but Tuesday took its name from Tisa the wife of Thor, Wednesday from Woden, Thursday from Thor himself, Friday from Freya, the beautiful daughter of Niord, and Saturday from Saeter. And all of them had to be treated with respect or the worst would happen.

Scotland's cockle and mussel gatherers also had their weekday superstitions. The tasty bivalve mollusc, the cockle – the shell symbol of which was the badge worn in pilgrims' hats – had to be collected on Monday, Tuesday and Wednesday morning, to be boiled on Wednesday and Thursday, and sold on Friday for the best results; any other arrangement would drive the cockles away said the superstitious. The mussel gatherers of the Eden rivermouth in Fife, had a similar ritual; they collected the mussel scallops as bait and injudicious collection would bring bad luck to the fishermen who used them.

Of all the months, **May** has the most superstitions attached to it. Bad luck would follow the making of household brooms, or besoms, in May; and a broom made of birch twigs, or green broom should never be used in May because it would sweep away the family luck for a generation. Eggs set under hens in May would not hatch out they said in the Borders. To wash blankets in May was ill-omened too, for to do so 'washes one of the family away' (i.e., it was a death omen).

In some parts of Scotland, kittens born in May were deemed far more languid and were drowned at birth for no more reason than their birth date. May kittens were thought weakly and unlikely to grow into strong vermin-catching cats. Such kittens would also bring snakes and slow-worms into the house, and when they were older they would lie on the faces of babies in the cradle and suffocate them. In Ross and Cromarty they said that May cats sucked the breath of children and caused their death.

Almost universally in Scotland, May was deemed the worst month to get married: 'Marry in May, rue for aye' ran the old saw. Scotland buzzed with superstitious gossip when Mary Queen of Scots announced that she would marry Henry Stuart, Lord Darnley, in May. the English Principal Secretary William Cecil, Lord Burghley, reminded the court what he had said about the ill-fated marriage of the Earl of Leicester and Amy Robsart – *Nuptiae carnales a laetitia incipiunt et in luctu terminantur* ('Carnal marriages begin with happiness and end in strife') carnality being the curse of May liaisons. Indeed, on Mary's wedding day someone pinned this note to a door in the Canongate, Edinburgh; 'Only wantons marry in the month of May'. It was Mary's wedding, by the by, that reminded folk of some of the old **wedding** superstitions. Had the old folk not also said it was unlucky to marry in **January**, too, when the year was too new, and how it was necessary to avoid a dog passing between bride and groom? Between the announcement of the marriage ceremony and the ceremony itself, the friends of the bride would rub shoulders with her, for if they were unmarried, it would help them catch the matrimonial 'infection'.

The celebration of returning fertility, and its supposed magical stimulation, is the basis for all Scottish superstitions associated with **Spring**, the season of drinking, feasting, dancing and lovemaking.

Spring was a time too when old scores could be settled with the maximum chance of success. At Candlemas (2 February, the medieval festival of the Purification of the Blessed Virgin Mary, when candles were lit and blessed), gatherings of men would assemble at the Border with the intent of nocturnal raids into England. This old tradition is remembered each year at Jedburgh, when the Ba' Game takes place. Two teams pursue a ball through the ancient burgh. Custom calls for the ball to have streamers which, it is said, represent the severed heads of the rapacious English invaders who harried the Borders for centuries.

At Lanark the Whuppity Stourie custom during **March**, is deemed to be a superstitious welcome to Spring. 'Whuppity Stourie' is quoted as the name of an evil spirit which had to be dispelled with a fight. Today children race round the town whirling paper balls in the air, which represent the artifacts of old, once thrown to dispel the evil. The old explanation said that during Spring the evil spirits travelled in clouds of stour (dust) and blighted the sown crops. If you threw your left shoe, or your hat – or a naked knife, or earth from a mole cast – at the dust clouds it would prevent the evil spirits from carrying out their malignant intention.

The symbol of **Summer**, the sun, attracted to it some interesting superstitions in Scotland. Lucky is the bride that the sun shines on – the superstitious said it would make her fruitful like the planted fields – and anyone could attract good luck if they did a sunwise turn before attempting a new project. To point at the sun, however, was to encourage disaster. The key was to make a *deiseil* turn – towards the sun's path – on your heel for success. To go *widdershins* (against the sun's path) strengthened the powers of darkness. This is why, the superstitious said, sailors of old always passed the port 'clockwise' (i.e., *deiseil*).

The folklorists noted how, on Lewis in late summer, when they brought the cattle to their winter pasture, the farmers guarded their beasts, from illness by paying a man to run three times around the herd carrying a lighted torch in his hand and running from east to west. Should any beast have hurt its leg in the high pastures it could be cured by leading it three times sunwise round an ancient stone. Three times was always the magic number here, and the folk of Lothian once said that should a man run *widdershins* three times round a church he would see the Devil peering at him from the porch.

'The haunt o' Spring's the primrose brae,
The Summer joys the flocks to follow.
How cheery thro' her shortening day,
Is Autumn in her weeds o' yellow!'

So sang Robert Burns in *By Allan Stream* (1793) reflecting on the time when Scots folk began to think of decay and the passage of the seasons for **Autumn** in Scotland was a period of introspection about the closing year. In many country districts it was considered unlucky to tell one's age at any time of year, but in Autumn the old counting superstitions were at their most potent.

In Scotland Autumn was the period of Lammas, the Celtic festival of harvested fruit and crops, when all of the bounty of the soil was celebrated. All over Scotland in pre-Reformation times, towns, villages and hamlets celebrated with bonfires, races and games, and the old folk said it was the best time for marriages. So Lammas was the season of handfasting, when lovers plighted their troth by grasping each other's hand through a holed stone (the relics of prehistoric man) like the holed Stone of Odin, Stenness, Orkney, made famous by Sir Walter Scott in his book *The Pirate*. An Autumn marriage, said the old folk, was the strongest of all.

In Scotland, **Winter**, the season of wet, darkness and cold has traditionally been the time when free rein has been given to fantasy. As families huddled round the ingle-neuk it was the season to listen to the sagas and folktales. Everyone knew that Winter was the Season of Ghosts, and throughout Northern Europe it was the moment to celebrate the Cult of the Dead, hallowed by the Saxons in Autumn, and the Celts in Midwinter. These rites were absorbed by Christianity within All Saints' Day (1 Nov) and All Souls (2 Nov).

Because it symbolised the sun, and gave warmth, fire has perhaps the most superstitious lore when associated with Winter. Most of Scotland's winter festivals, from the Burning of the Clavie in Burghhead to Comrie's Flambeau Procession, reflect these old superstitions, for if the sun did not come back all was lost for the world.

Rain, Clouds and Sunshine

THE idea that winds can speak warnings of impending doom, or that certain storms only occur when royalty is taken ill, sound strange to the modern ear; but once a belief in them was common in Scotland. Otta F. Swire, the collector of old Scottish legends, noted one curious weather story.

It was November 1928 and Otta Swire was at Kingsburgh, near Loch Snizort, Beag, Skye. At Buckingham Palace, King George V was seriously ill with a streptococcal infection of the chest, and every evening an old Skye man came to the house at Kingsburgh to hear on the radio the latest broadcast news of the King. The old man had been a stalker in his youth and had served the King in that capacity at Balmoral when George was Prince of Wales. Around the 24 November there was a day of wild, strong winds, snow and thunder on Skye, which raged for hours until the evening when the gales abated. In the gloaming the old man came as usual to Kingsburgh and asked if the King was still alive. On being told that George lived, he went away.

The old man did not return; and when he was later informed that the King had taken a step towards recovery the old man nodded that he knew, for the King had not gone with the storm. The tempest had been a 'Royal Storm', he said, a squall that only blew for 'great ones'. The old man had seen such a storm which had come in 1916 and taken Earl Kitchener of Khartoum with it. But this storm had gone without the King, so he knew that the monarch would recover.

To Scotland's ingenuous forebears the world was a place full of sorcery, and above all things in the scale of importance were the phenomena of Nature which brought and then took away the rain and the snow, the wind and the hail. On all these things depended the crops and the way of life of the seamen, the huntsmen and the husbandmen.

So wherever you go in Scotland there are relics of the old superstitions about **weather**, often set in proverbs and rhymes. Here is one example from the Lothians:

A frosty winter and a dusty March, and a rain about Averil: *April*
Another about the Lammas time when the corn begins to fill,   *1 Aug*
Is worth a plough of gold and all her pins theretill.

In Yarrow they said:

'If the evening is red and the morning is grey,
It is the sign of a bonnie day.
If the evening's grey and the morning red,
The lamb and the ewe will go wet to bed.'

In Tweedside they pinpointed certain months:

'February, an ye be fair,
The hoggs 'ill mend and naething pair;
                              Year-old sheep/lessen
February and ye be foul,
The hoggs 'ill die in ilka pool.'   *every*

In Morayshire they settled for the actions of geese:

'Wild geese, wild geese, ganging to the sea,
Good weather it will be.
Wild geese, wild geese, ganging to the hill,
The weather it will spill.'

Down the East Coast the seamen had their own weather lore:

'Hen's scarts and mares' tails   *scratchings*
Make lofty ships carry low sails.'

and

'If the rain comes before the wind,
Lower your topsails and take them in.
If the wind comes before the rain,
Lower your topsails and hoist them again.'

17

At some time before mankind began to observe the weather for positive clues to help hunting and agriculture, Scotland's tribesmen believed that they could do something to control the weather. So to the tribal shaman was given the task of estimating the wind, the clouds, the flight of birds and the colour of the sky, as well as the enactment of rituals to turn evil portents into good ones.

Perhaps it was the Noreseman who first gave Scotland her superstitious weather-lore, for they were interested in the sympathetic magic which stilled the sea storm and tamed the flood. On Uist, in the Hebrides, for instance, a stone-cross, called the Water Cross, stood opposite St Mary's church, and this cross was used in weather control. When rain was required the cross was raised; in time of flood, the cross was lowered again.

Sir Walter Scott studied weather-lore when he wrote his book *The Pirate*. He gleaned his information during his trip in 1814 with the Commissioners for the Northern Lighthouse Service around the Scottish islands. In particular he was intrigued by the stories of King Eric of Sweden who was deemed able to control the wind by altering the direction of his cap. To change the bearing of the wind, Eric turned his cap in the direction he wanted; thus was the King called 'Windy Cap'.

By far the most Scottish lore on weather is concerned with omens, and naturally enough the superstitions about climate are most common in the rural districts. Country folk believed that if cattle feed vigorously all together, or lie down in low-lying pasturage, that rain is coming. On the contrary, if they rest on high pastures then the weather will be fine. Amongst the families of the Border hill-farms sheep were given a similar set of superstitions. If the sheep were restless or bleated loudly for no logical reason heavy rain was predicted.

Country folk, too, read weather lore into the movements of the leaves on their trees. Should leaves make a sudden rustling noise then rain was not far off. The same was said of leaves which unexpectedly turned their undersides to the sky. Perhaps the best known Scottish weather superstition connected with trees is the one rhyming the first appearance of oak and ash leaves.

18

'If the Oak comes before the Ash,
 We shall only have a splash.
 If the Ash comes before the Oak,
 We are sure to have a soak.'

For centuries people have seen omens in their house fires, detected from the behaviour of the fire in the grate. Should the flames of the family fire burn blue then frost was predicted; the same was said if a candle flame took on a blue tinge.

A black snail crossing anyone's path is a sure sign of rain, the old folk said, but many put most trust in the best respected weather-prophet of all, the **hedgehog**. For centuries the old Scots country folk believed that the hedgehog knew when storms were coming and sensed the direction of an ensuing wind. The weather superstitions of the hedgehog were set out by *Poor Robin's Almanack* for the edition of 1733 under the name of Poor Robin, Knight of the Burnt-Island:

'Observe which way the hedgehog builds her nest,
 To front the north or south, or east or west;
 For if 'tis true that common people say,
 The wind will blow the quite contrary way.

If by some secret art the hedgehogs know
 So long before, which way the winds will blow,
 She has an art which many a person lacks,
 That thinks himself fit to make almanacks.'

Before street lights blanked out for most the beauties of **moonlight**, it too was regarded as a weather predictor. In the Highlands and the Western Isles, women curtseyed and men doffed their bonnets to the **moon** in honour of the great respect they had for its powers. As the moon waxed and waned, so would climate and growing things be affected. Some planted their crops to suit the phases of the moon, and others pruned their fruit trees during another phase to take advantage of the moon's beneficence. A new moon rising on a Saturday or Sunday meant bad weather to come. And, some said, that two moons in a single month meant four weeks continuing squalls; yet 'two moons in May means rain for a year and a day'.

The moon also had another set of superstitions attributed to it. It was thought unlucky to see a new moon for the first time through a window, or if your hands were empty at the time. To have something in your hands when you saw the new moon for the first time meant that you were to receive a substantial present before the moon had waned. And money in the pocket must be turned at the first sight of a new moon, to assure a plentiful supply of it for a whole year.

A pig to be slaughtered for salt pork must be killed before a moon was on the increase, else the meat would not keep well. And fish hung in the moonlight would develop poisonous properties.

Sleeping in the moonlight was thought to cause madness; and in the Scottish Borders if you slept with the moon streaming through your window onto your face it was said this would cause you to develop a twisted mouth.

A new moon on a Saturday was said to forecast bad weather, but a good harvest was forecast if such an event took place only once in seven years, as the Aberdeenshire rhyme averred:

'A Saiterday meen an' a Sunday's prime
Gehn she cum ance in saiven year
She comes in gueede time.'

Clouds feature quite often in weather-lore rhymes. From Fife come these:

'When Largo Law the mist doth bear
Let Kellie Law for storms prepare.'

and

'When Falkland Hill puts on his cap
The Howe o'Fife will get a drap.'

In Roxburghshire lore two other peaks were specified:

'When Ruberslaw puts on his cowl
The Dunian on his hood
Then a' the wives of Teviotside
Ken there will be a flood.'

In the Highlands should a mountain not have a cap of clouds, but a collar of them instead, wherein the peak appeared through the clouds, then it was time to climb up and divest oneself of evil spirits. As you climbed through the cloud and out into the sunshine you would leave the evil spirits behind you choked in the clouds.

There were two interesting types of **weather days** in Scotland, 'flatterin'' and 'borrowing'. Thus a Friday that is fine during a period of wet weather in Aberdeenshire was called a 'flatterin' Friday', for it indicated a lengthening of the wet weather.

'Borrowing days' were the last three days of March, said to be 'borrowed' from April as is shown in the folk-rhyme:

'March borrowed from April
Three days, and they were ill;
The first it wiz sna' an' sleet,
The second it wiz cauld and weet,
The third it wiz sic a freeze,
The birds' nebs stack t'the trees.'

February also had 'borrowed' days, the 12,13 and 14 borrowed from January, and superstitious people forecast that if they be stormy, the rest of the year would be favoured with good weather; but, should they be fine, then the year would be foul and unfavourable for farmers. The country folk called them *faoilteach* days, and hence *faoilteach*, became to mean dreadful weather.

Mystic Hues and Secret Numbers

SCOTS have always believed that there was a spiritual-
ity about colours which gave them a connection with
physical things: **white**, for instance, was thought cold,
and **red** was considered hot. In pre-Reformation Scotland, a common cure for neck-ache and whooping
cough was to wear a scarlet scarf, and so potently
good was red that witches hated it. In 1904 a Glasgow
pharmacist's catalogue listed 'Crimson Salt' as the 'best
disinfectant in the world'; at 1/- (5p) a bottle it was adver-
tised as curing anything from skin diseases to gout. In
reality it was nothing more than dyed common salt,
but the red colouring played on the superstitious beliefs
concerning the efficacy of red medicine.

The colour of objects then was speculated as mystic,
and no more curious Scottish story linking colour with
mystic healing is to be found than the tale of the **Black
Lee Penny**. This object furnished Sir Walter Scott with
an idea for his book *The Talisman* (1825) wherein the
Scottish hero, Earl David of Huntingdom, is disguised
as Sir Kenneth, Knight of the Leopard, and is given a
sacred amulet by Sultan Saladin of Egypt.

Sir Walter introduced the historical base for his story;
Robert I, the Bruce, had died in 1329, never fulfilling
his desire to visit the Holy Land in pious pilgrimage,
but before his death he had asked his friend Sir James
Douglas to take his heart to the Holy Land and fight the
infidel.

Thus Bruce's dead heart was placed in a silver casket
by Sir James and the key to the casket was carried by
Sir Symon Locard (Lockhart) of Lee. The Scots knights
encountered the Moors on the crusade route through
Spain, and Sir James was killed as he carried Bruce's
heart into battle at Tiba, near Granada in 1330.

The Scots knights returned to Scotland and Bruce's
heart was buried at Melrose Abbey, Sir Symon Locard
returning to his estates with a ransom purse containing

money and a precious amulet which – Sir Walter Scott said in his introduction to *The Talisman* – had been used to ransom a saracen Emir at Granada. Today that stone amulet, called the Lee Penny, remains in the possession of the Lockhart family of Lee, and has long been used as an amulet to cure bleeding, the bites of mad dogs and sickness in cattle and horses.

Set in an Edward IV groat (an English silver coin worth fourpence) the amulet is a dull, dark-red to black stone about an inch square, and is fastened to a short chain. The stone is kept in a gold snuff box presented to General James Lockhart by Marie Therese, Habsburg Empress of Austria in 1789.

To set the cure in motion the stone should be dipped three times in water; the liquid then becomes a curative agent the superstitious said. Records show that the coin set amulet was used in epidemics of cattle disease in Haddington, Newcastle and Lancashire to great effect. According to *The Scots Magazine* of 1787, the most noteworthy cure was enacted on Lady Baird of Sauchtonhall, who was cured of hydrophobia by the Lee Penny after being bitten by a mad dog; she lived to be a venerable age.

Mary Queen of Scots also used the symbolism of the colour red to great effect. As she doffed her outer dress a few minutes before she was beheaded at Fotheringay Castle in 1587 she revealed an under dress of dark red, the liturgical colour of martyrdom in the Roman church; no one assembled in the great hall mistook its significance.

Many summed up their beliefs in the old rhyme:

'Blue is true and for affection,
Yellow's jealous and false.
Green's forsaken and full of hope,
Red is brazen with health and strength
While rose marks a sweet disposition.
White is pure in love
As orange is for luxury.
Violet's for intelligence
And lilac for freshness.
But black is for death.'

Blue the colour of fidelity still appears in the wedding rhyme . . . 'something blue . . .', but a despised colour in medieval Scotland was **yellow** the colour of serfs and bankrupts.

The colour of night and darkness, and therefore evil, death and the Devil, black has the worst superstitious lore. But **green** has more folkloric associations than any other colour for it was the 'colour of the fairies'. It must be said too that green was commonly known in Scotland as the colour of envy, and undoubtedly this sentiment is behind two old Scots customs – if a girl was married before her older sisters she gave them green stockings; and in Fife knitted green garters were secretly fastened to the clothes of an older unmarried brother or sister of a bride.

Coloured designs traced in pipeclay on thresholds, the floors of houses, dairies and byres were once very common in Scotland to keep away ghosts. Tangled threads, stars and prickly plants in red, green and yellow were the most popular motifs. As late as 1934, the folklorist M.M. Banks was recording such designs 'in the cottage of a shepherd near Melrose'. The shepherd's wife was a Lanarkshire woman, who had 'been in service in dairies in Ayrshire'; her designs were traced fresh every morning on the thresholds of house and byre, hearth and cobbled stable floor and on milk-pans. She did not know why she did it but when she had worked in Ayrshire it had been a necessary part of her job, for it would bring good luck to the workplace.

Some believe that the whorls and squiggles were direct relics of the cup-and-ring markings which were carved into rock by the barbarians of the second millenium in Scotland's Border Country. What the markings mean is very much a matter of conjecture today, and may have been a part of the mystique of the metal-using craftsmen of the day. The meaning of more modern markings was clear though, a great desire to keep away evil from hearth and home, goods and food.

Despite the fact that the **tartan** as a national dress of Scotland is quite modern in concept, the colourful *breacan* (Gaelic for tartan, meaning 'chequered'), has

a direct link with Scottish colour lore. It is thought that
the tartans used hundreds of years ago in the Highlands
were of simple checks of two or three colours made
from dyes of plants, roots, berries and trees. Thus the
original tartans were not family designs but district motifs
from the location of the vegetable dyes.

In the sixteenth century they were making cloth at
Narraboll, Islay, of white, black and green colours –
hues considered very lucky in the area. Those 'lucky'
colours probably make up the oldest tartan known and
are the shades used in the tartan of the Macleans of
Duart.

When the Lamont clan lands around Toward and
Ascog castles were ravaged by the Campbell chieftains,
the clansmen looked to the 'lucky colours' of the clan
for new names; thus **brown**, black, and white feature
as modern surnames represented by the Lamont clan.

Perhaps the 'unlucky' colours of **orange** and green in
Scotland may take their sinister attributes from the fact
that they were the hues of Druids' ceremonial robes.
Some Scottish unions used colourful costumes for their
'trade mysteries'; for instance the Bakers Union of Aberdeen wore **pink** muslin suits at their meetings topped
with turbans.

'Nine days' wonder' and 'Nine lives of a cat' are old
enough adages, but the figure **nine** has more local rele-
vance in Scotland when related to the playing card the
Nine of Diamonds. There are a number of reasons why
this card is picked out as 'The Curse of Scotland'.

Some said that one, George Campbell, tried to steal
the state crown of Scotland but only managed to steal
nine diamonds from it. A tax was subsequently laid on
the people of Scotland to replace the diamonds and that
burden was called 'the curse of Scotland'.

Others said that the curse was associated with the
Massacre of Glencoe. It's an oft-told tale that early in
his reign, William III summoned all the Scottish Highland Chiefs to take an oath of allegiance to him. The
Macdonalds failed to do so. Owing to a misunderstand-
ing, a royal warrant was issued to 'root out that damna-
ble sept' and the Campbells, the hereditary foes of the

Macdonalds, were sent to carry it out – by trickery they massacred the whole clan at Glencoe in 1692. Some said that Sir John Dalrymple of Stair, Secretary of State, used a playing card, the nine of diamonds, to sign his assent for the massacre; significantly, said others, the heraldic shield of the Dalrymples displays diamonds.

Still others put forward the idea that before the Battle of Culloden in 1746 Charles Edward Stuart was playing cards with the Laird of Macintosh at his Inverness house. The Nine of Diamonds was dropped from the table and lost. Some time later when the Duke of Cumberland stayed at the house the card was found and the noble duke used it to authorise a death warrant.

'The eleventh hour' (or 'just in time' from the parable in *Matthew* 20) still has an ominous ring as does the 'twelve arrows'. The latter comes from an old saw that 'Each English archer carries twelve Scotsmen under his girdle' meaning that as the English were unerring archers each carried **twelve** Scots lives in the belt where they held their arrows.

Thirteen is the most universally regarded unlucky number of all; the Christians attributing it to the thirteen who sat down at the Last Supper and the pagans to the Spirit of Mischief, Loki, who was the thirteenth guest at the banquet in Valhalla. Is this why many hostesses don't like having thirteen guests at dinner today? Friday 13 of any month is still considered unlucky all over Scotland.

Scotland's early philosophers knew that belief which was given substance in the time of the Greek philosopher Pythagoras, that all numbers and their multiples had a mystic significance, and that the numbers one to thirteen had particular power. Numbers were thought too, to be the underlying structure of God's universe, and as with names (see page 52) numbers were a private part of a person's character and journey through life. So personal were numbers that it is probable that half-remembered memories about numbers and not vanity is the reason why some people will not reveal their age.

In medieval times **one** was the number of God the Father, and **two** of his opponent the Devil; **three** was the Trinity, **four** the earth and solidity and **five** the flesh and so on. But some numbers like, 3, 7, 9, 12, 22, 40 and 70 were the numbers of 'completeness' and played an important role in Scottish mysticism and magic. There's luck in odd numbers said the folk of the Mearns.

It was common gossip that good and bad luck had a threefold aspect. So, should an accident befall you, it was very likely that two more disasters would follow, especially if you saw two clergymen together. Around Garioch they used to say that if there was a funeral in the parish then two more would follow within a month. Thus visitors, gifts and letters were affirmed as coming in threes, and two objects broken in a house would be followed by a third. Old charms were often repeated three times for efficacy and, as it was a most fortunate numeral, that is why old Scots said 'three times lucky'.

The unwary were warned that it was very unlucky to light three candles from the same taper, or have three lights on in a room. Strangely, this superstition returned to Scotland during World War I when, during trench warfare, it was considered unlucky to light three cigarettes from the one match (it gave an enemy sniper time to shoot the third man).

No-one could hear your gossip they said in Banff if you said 'within four walls'. **Seven**, linked with the ages of man, was a number of great mystic significance in Scotland. For instance a seventh child was the one most denied natural gifts in a family, but seven horseshoes nailed to a front door was the best of all guards against evil. Every seventh and ninth year of life was thought to bring either great change or danger, as was the age of **sixty-three** (seven multiplied by nine); if a man or woman survived sixty-three unassailed by evil he or she would live to a ripe old age.

Birds of Fortune and Insects of Destiny

MAN has always coveted the birds' ability to fly, an act which brought them into contact with the sky powers and the realm of the gods. The idea that birds were bringers of news from supernatural sources dates from the stories of Noah. Because of their affinity with man, walking on two legs, dancing, preening and home building, birds have a special place in Scotland's superstitious lore.

The most vocal of all creatures, man and birds were long thought to be able to communicate verbally one with another, and once it was deemed that a **hawk's** tongue placed under the human tongue would give the power to speak with the birds. Indeed the famous ballad *The Twa Corbies* gives a reference to a person 'walking all alone' overhearing **crows** discuss their grisly repast on the corpse of a knight.

The crow, incidentally, with its rusty black plumage was associated with death and disaster, as well as being the wily confidant of the gods. All Scottish superstition concerning crows seems to stem from the Celtic myths and the days of Odin, bynamed Hrafna-gud, 'god of the raven'. And in highland folklore the feared Cailleach, appears as a hooded-crow to wreak devastation on the unwary.

To see a single crow was thought unlucky, and to hear one croaking to your left as you went out into the fields in the morning was a very ill-omen. Should a crow flutter against a house windowpane, this was considered a death warning; and four flying over a house forecast sorrow for the family therein, while two indicated a wedding or a birth.

The **raven** was also a bird of ill-fortune in Scotland and is remembered too, as a creature sacred to Odin, who had two attendant ravens, Hugin and Munin, who brought him back news of the world's happenings. To hear a raven croak before you set off on a journey was very bad luck, but some were not perturbed as they believed that the raven contained the soul of King Arthur. Condemned to be black and eat carrion because it did not return to Noah's ark with the message that the 'waters were dried up from off the earth', the raven would turn anyone's hair black who ventured to eat its eggs.

Because of the distinctive cry of the **cuckoo**, the bird has been considered one which showed the gift of prophecy, especially as it announces the coming of Spring with such enthusiasm. In Scotland's islands though, it was considered unlucky to hear the cuckoo before breakfast because it brought bad luck for the rest of the day. The bird is also known as the messenger of Thor, the Scandinavian god in whose gift were happy marriages, but some looked upon the cuckoo as a rain-bird and a bringer of warm weather after showers. In the northern counties of Scotland, where the cuckoo is known as the *Gowk*, a 'gowk-storm' is the rough weather foretold by its song. Another storm-bird, this time of the Shetlands, is the red-throated **diver** whose cries are deemed to forecast a spell of wet weather.

Some people don't like the cuckoo because it lays its eggs in other birds' nests for them to hatch, and 'sucks little birds' eggs to make its voice clear' says the old ballad.

The size, strength and aristocratic bearing of the **eagle** has given it a unique place in Scottish superstition and probably the beliefs that the eagle's feathers are incorruptible made it the magic symbol of longevity. The folk of the Shiant Isles, in the Hebrides, extended this superstition to aver that Adam and Eve continued to live on in the Highlands as eagles.

It is said to be very unlucky to rob an eagle's nest, whosoever does so will be haunted for the rest of their lives, knowing no rest. Many Scots took the risk, however, in the hope of finding an eagle-stone in the nest. This was the name given to the small light brown aetites (*lapis acquilaris*) much sought as amulets against miscarriages and for protection during pregnancy. An eagle's egg, too, if shared by two people would protect them against witchcraft. Should those with bad eyesight eat the gall of eagles mixed with honey, then they would have their sight restored.

That strange whistling noise made by the golden **plover** was said by some to give warning to sheep of danger nearby, but the **lapwing**'s cry is likened to the ill-omened clamour of 'Bewitched! Bewitched!' as befits a bird deemed a departing spirit of a dead human. The cry of the **yellowhammer**, known in Scotland as the yellow-yorling, was compared to a devilish screech; the old proverbs said that the bird 'will drink a drop of the Devil's blood every May Day'. In Scotland the yorling's cry was a fancied mimicking of the human voice:

'Whetil te, whetil te, whae.
 Harry my nest and the de'il tak' ye.'

Leave a **rook**'s nest alone too, the old folk said, for it is bad luck for all in a parish if a rookery is destroyed or threatened.

Certain birds are particularly beloved of the gods the old rhymes tell us. That streetwise comedian the squabbling **sparrow** is one; as a guide to the souls of the dead seeking rest, it was thought unlucky if a sparrow flew into a house and could not get out again. The **swan** is another loved bird, the incarnation of the Swan-maiden of European legend, whose eggs needed thunder and lightning to hatch. In old Scot's lore it was recounted that anyone who harmed a swan would die within a year.

They will tell you in Dumfriesshire that the **blackbird** was once white. It turned black when it took refuge one cold winter in the devil's chimney; so if you run into a pale coloured blackbird then watch your step.

Coal miners in Scotland's central belt do not like to see **pigeons** flying around a pithead as they are then bad-luck omens. And it's very bad luck to stuff pillows or cushions with the feathers of pigeons or doves.

The **wren** has a mixed reception in Scotland. Some said it was the favourite bird of Druidic soothsayers in past days. Indeed because of this the early Christian missionaries hated the bird and it was often hunted and killed. There is a belief in southwest Scotland that if a wren is killed deliberately, the local cows will give blood instead of milk. Others believe that if you kill a wren or destroy its nest then you will break a limb in the coming year. The wren was particularly disliked by Highlanders who said that it was the bird who told the enemies of Christ in which direction He fled.

As a night bird, the **owl** with its eerie-sounding cries is one held by country folk of old with superstitious fear. The witches of *Macbeth* used an owlet's wing to give their concoctions potency, and in the far north of Scotland owl's meat was deemed a good cure for hangovers and epilepsy. To see an owl at midday, or hear it hooting in the afternoon was an evil omen. To avert ill-luck on such an occasion it was wise to put a knot in your handkerchief; some even threw a handful of salt onto the fire.

Perhaps the most popular bird in Scottish superstition is the **robin**, and certainly it has the oldest references. It is first mentioned in the twelfth century biography of St Kentigern, Bishop of Glasgow (*d.* AD 601). The chronicler tells us that St Kentigern's teacher had a pet robin which came daily to perch on his shoulder or head, and that some rumbustuous boys handled it so roughly that it died. St Kentigern restored it to life and the robin is still depicted on the coat of arms of the city of Glasgow, Kentigern's own town. The robin has traditional associations with blood and fire, indeed colours have long been linked with birds:

Red – fire, lightning, blood – the **chough**'s red beak set fire to things.

Yellow – cure for jaundice – you would be cured if looked at by a stone **curlew**'s yellow eye.

Black – evil/witches –' bad weather would destroy crops if the **jackdaw** came home late in the evening.

White – portent of death – the **nightjar** was called the 'corpse tender' by some Scots, particularly if piebald nightjars were seen in cemeteries.

All pied birds were bringers of confusion and none more than the **wagtail** and **magpie**.

The magpie has always been regarded in Scotland as sinister and mysterious, undoubtedly because of its black and white plumage. In northeast Scotland the magpie was always 'the Dei'l's bird' and was thought to have a drop of the devil's blood under its tongue. Hence the rhyme . . .

'One for sorrow, two for mirth,
Three for a wedding, four for a birth,
Five for silver, six for gold,
Seven for a secret not to be told;
Eight for heaven, nine for hell,
And ten for the devil himsel'.'

Because of its loud raucous voice the magpie was believed to take up human speech, the old folk averred, if the reddest area of its tongue be scratched and a drop of human blood be inserted. Indeed, it was observed that magpies in captivity were able to mimic human sounds. Some farmers even used magpies as watch-dogs; for from their cages they would create a din if a stranger or a predatory animal came by.

In the southwest of Scotland it was unlucky to see a magpie flying away from the sun. Should someone do so, they should immediately seize something to throw after the bird with the chant: 'Bad luck to the bird that

nd Mountain

shadows, the **bat** is pre-
wings and hideous facial
y supernatural skill of hunt-
s, the bat has a frightening
tion to its size. Its supposed
been known in Scotland
and as a tool of the Devil.
power in a hell-brew when
ion of the Weird Sisters of the
eth:

e of frog,
ongue of dog.'

uscript there is the note that when
wards to then dive swiftly down to
about with the power over human
o precautions against them.

gent of the Devil, or cherished as a
fortune and health, the domestic **cat**
history in Scotland. Certainly until the
hteenth century cats were burned alive
ds at the ritual fire called *taigheirin*, to
e Celtic gods the power of the second
land it is a white cat that is the embodi-
, with the black cat – which should be
ed along its spine to ensure good luck –
benign magic. For a black cat to cross your
emely lucky (if it does so from right to left).
ts observed cats as a guide to weather lore: a
g cat forecast high winds, but one sitting with
o the fire foretold of frost; should a cat wash its
rain was to be expected.

cat has been associated with witchcraft in Scot-
nce the days when the two crazed Dominican
James Sprenger and Heinrich Kramer wrote
ti-witch nonsense *Malleus Malificarum* (1484).

38

flies widdershins'. It was always thought bad luck to encounter magpies at the beginning of a journey.

Other 'devil birds' are the **swifts** said to be 'the souls of the damned' condemned to fly over the places they inhabited in mortal life for their misdeeds. **Swallows** have this dark reputation too, for like the magpie they were also said to carry a drop of the devil's blood under their tongues, and, in the days when coal fires were popular, if a swallow fell down your chimney in a cloud of soot a death in the family was forecast.

Of farmyard birds Scots folklore says this. The Norsemen believed that the dawn of Ragnnarok – the Christian Doomsday – would be signalled by the crowing of a gold-crested **rooster**, and for this pagan reason the cock is a bird of many superstitions in Scotland. It is a death omen to hear a cock crow three times between sunset and midnight, but a cock crowing near a house door – or crowing indoors – foretells the coming of unexpected visitors or strangers.

Some newly married couples were given a **hen** to carry into their first home; if it crowed loudly it was a sign of good luck. Others said it was a sign of future petticoat rule!

Farmers in Angus and the Mearns hung dead **ducks** head-down to hasten the departure of evil spirits from a farmhouse. And, it was said that if duck eggs were taken into a house after dark they would never hatch.

Scotland followed other northern European countries in believing that **butterflies** were a symbol of the soul, and to see one flying at night was a warning of an impending death. In Gaelic tradition those newly-dead were thought to be sometimes visible in the form of a butterfly fluttering over the corpse. A golden butterfly hovering over the dead was a good omen of his or her life in the beyond. The larva of a butterfly, the caterpillar, was deemed as the creature of the Devil made as a helper of witches in concocting potions; but to carry one around was supposed to be a cure for fever.

Country folk often said that if **ants** were particularly busy, then bad weather was nigh. It was considered bad luck to kill a **ladybird** for it was often used in

35

fortune-telling. Girls in search of a lover ~
the insect on the back of the hand and ~

'Flee, ladybird, north, south, east or we~
Flee where the man is found that I lo'e b~

While children chanted:

'Ladybird, ladybird, fly away home,
Your house is on fire and your children are
gone . . .
All except one and that's little Ann
And she has crept under the warming pan.'

If the ladybird flew away, rain was to be expected; but there would be thunder and lightning if you killed a **beetle**. Should any beetle fall on its back it was lucky to turn it over.

There's many an old wives' tale about **spiders** in Scotland, from fever being cured if you wore a spider in a nutshell around your neck, to wounds being healed by the application of a spider's web. Spiders in a house were always thought luck omens, and a money-spider placed in a purse ensured that this owner would never be without cash. Every child could recite the story of how Robert I, the Bruce, while on the island of Rathlin, Antrim, watched a spider try six times to fix its web to a beam. Bruce took this as a sign to continue his own struggles against defeat. Thus encouraged Bruce left the island to triumph and become the virtual master of Scotland. For good measure the old balladists quoted the rhyme:

'If ye wish take live lang and thrive
Let a spider run alive.'

It was once thought a mortal sin to kill **bees**, the tiny winged servants of God. For this reason their folklore in Scotland underlines their having knowledge of the future and being wise. Anger or hatred in a household would drive them away, nor do they like blasphemy near their hives, or unchastity, the old folk said.

A bee entering a house was a sign of very good luck; indeed announcing the coming of a stranger bearing

Animals of Field a~

OF ALL the creatures of the ~
eminent. With its leather-lik~
appearance and its apparent ~
ing its prey in total darkne~
reputation out of all propo~
occult powers have lon~
as a familiar of witches ~
Shakespeare knew of its ~
he wrote of the concoc~
deserted heath in Macb~

'Eye of wolf and to~
Wool of bat and t~

In the Wilkie Man~
bats in flight rise up~
earth, witches are ~
beings who take ~

Feared as an ~
bringer of good ~
has had a mixe~
close of the ei~
in the Highlan~
secure from ~
sight. In Sco~
ment of evi~
gently strok~
symbolising~
path is ext~
Many Sco~
scamperi~
its back ~
ears the~

The ~
land ~
mo~
th~

Everyone knew that cats were the familiars of witches, so no-one was surprised that the witch Isobel Grierson, who was strangled and burned at Castlehill, Edinburgh, in 1607, admitted that she had entered the house of Adam Clark at Prestonpans in the form of a cat.

We learn most about the superstitions associated with animals and witches in Scotland from such cases as that of Isobel Gowdie of Auldearne, Morayshire, who publicly declared herself a witch in 1662. She claimed that she and other witches were able to turn themselves into **hares** and cats, and had power over animals to do their will; and they were able to turn **toads** into **oxen**.

The hare, incidentally, associated in myth with the moon, was a feared beast of ill-omen throughout Scotland; in the shape of a hare, a witch could be killed only by a silver bullet.

'If you see a white **horse** spit three times', says the old belief, and should you do that and wish a wish, that wish would be deemed to come true. Some say that this superstition is a memory of Scotland's crusader knights setting out for the Holy Land, but there are more curious superstitions in Scotland concerning horses.

The Celtic goddess, Epona, presided over horses and ponies, and would sometimes appear in their shape. So horses were worshipped in past days in Scotland and their bones were much prized for house protection; in particular, a horse's skull set into the gable of a house would protect that house from evil for generations. There is many a story too about horses being able to see ghosts. In his *Highland Folklore Heritage* Alexander Polson, writing in the 1920s, tells how he saw a carter's horse refuse to go by a certain gate; to all who were there, there was no sign of anything that might frighten the horse. The carter had to drag the horse past the gate, and the beast showed signs of much fear until it had cleared the opening. A few days later, Polson remembered, a corpse was carried through the same gateway on its way to the cemetery.

Even so the most curious superstitions of all concerning horses were to do with the mystic 'Horseman's Word'. This 'Word' was a secret charm which gave trained horsemen, from grooms to ploughmen, control over horses (and women). They only had to breathe the word into a horse's ear to make it do their bidding instantly. The belief in this was strongest in the north-east counties of Scotland and dated back beyond the Horsemen's Societies of medieval times and was born out of the ancient craft of horsemanship. At the age of 18 apprentice horsemen were initiated into the secret.

There is a belief in Scotland that the milk of a brown or red **cow** is better than that of a black or white. If the milkmaid did not wash her hands after milking the cow would run dry. Should a cow break into a walled garden, then it was an ill omen for the owner. In Scotland cows themselves were protected from evil by having rowan twigs braided into their tails with red thread. For many, a dry cow was a bewitched cow, but such an occurrence could be averted by tethering the beast with horsehair rope. The folklorist R.C. Maclagen told the tale of the farmer in Bernera who believed that his cows were bewitched, so he tethered them thus – with remarkable results; they began to give a plentitude of milk. Yet, when the beasts were released they all rushed over to a certain woman's house and began to toss their heads in her direction. This was regarded by the superstitious of Bernera that the woman had bewitched them. So strong was local feeling against her that she had to leave the district.

A howling **dog** heard at night has always been thought

of as a bad luck sign and gypsies did not like dogs digging holes near their encampment. A strange dog entering a house though, meant a new friendship to come soon they believed in the Highlands.

Despite the good luck brought by a hare and **rabbit** foot, these animals are almost always held in fear in Scotland. For a rabbit or a hare to cross your path on the way to market meant a disappointing deal that day.

Many old folk said that if the lambing season began with twins, the omens for a fertile season were good. If you met a flock of **sheep** on the road it was unlucky to part them. Again some folk in the Highlands used the blade-bone of a black sheep in divination. When the flesh was scraped off, the bone was placed in the house fire and the cracks which appeared during the burning process were thought to reveal the future, such as the lines of the hand revealed much to palmists.

Thunder, lightning and the tempestuous storm winds were all once associated with the wild **boar** in pagan Scotland. So the beliefs of the Norse and Celtic ancestors have given the Scots a variety of superstitions about **pigs**. For superstitious reasons many Highlanders were reluctant to eat pork because of the bad luck associated with the animal from which Our Lord had banished evil demons. But as pigs were deemed to be able to smell the wind, they were good weather prognosticators; should a pig run by with straw in its mouth then bad weather was forecast.

Consumption, warts, whooping cough and gout were all deemed to be cured by the application of **snail** slime: and a charm to know who one's future spouse would be was enacted using a snail on Hallowe'en. All you had to do was to imprison a snail overnight on a flat dish (i.e. the snail might be placed under an upturned bowl). Next morning, the superstitious said, the initials of the future wife or husband would be traced out on the dish's surface.

Dr George Henderson of Chirnside, Berwickshire, gave up much time for the study of Border rhymes and ballads. He was also interested in superstitions and jotted down these old beliefs as he travelled around the Border counties during the mid years of Victoria's reign:

Ass	It is said that the hairs from the tail of an ass are valuable cures for complaints of the limbs. (In the Highlands, by the by, a cure for a snakebite, or other stings, was to whisper into an ass's ear of your complaint and the pain would be transferred to the poor beast).
Fox	It's lucky to see one in the forenoon, but not in the afternoon.
Goat	He-goats are the favourite mounts of witches.
Mice	If mice suddenly vacate a house it indicates a death omen for someone living in the house.
Snakes	Can be kept away by raw onions, or ash branches.

It was the folk of the Borders, too, who believed that **hedgehogs** stole cows' milk by suckling from the beasts in the fields and many thought that they were more crafty and cunning than foxes. Should a garden not flourish, others said, because of poor soil, the thing to do was to spread around the fine soil from a fresh **mole** cast; this would make the old soil fertile.

Characters like Robert Louis Stevenson's 'Dr Jekyll and Mr Hyde' lie behind the myths of men having the power to change themselves into animals. But Scotland has its own mythical 'half-man-half-animal' creature in the **werewolf**. In traditional legend, the werewolf was a living person who had the magical power of changing his or her shape – and that shape in Scottish legend was usually the form of a wolf. There are some stories of other were-animals, like bears, but the wolf predominated in Scotland. Were (in werewolf) is, incidentally, the Old English word meaning man. Over the years it was a term of reproach in Scotland, to call anyone werewolf. Indeed in the records of the Presbytery of Kelso for 1660 there is a note that one John Broun, a weaver, was admonished for calling his neighbour by such a name.

The myth of the werewolf probably began in Scotland as a memory of the tribal worship of wolves. There were Scandinavian traditions in Scotland that the Norse Kings could transform themselves into animals. In Norse mythology, Fenris the wolf was the troublemaker in heaven and was deemed a child of the culture hero Loki. The werewolf came into focus in the Christian era's dark centuries of superstition and witch-hunting. By medieval times the folklore of Scotland had tied itself to an acknowledgement of the beast in man – that is, his worst nature – and that is where Dr Jekyll and Mr Hyde come in. Certainly, great thinkers like St Augustine and Cornelius Agrippa all believed in metamorphosis in general and lycanthropy in particular.

The association of the wolf with Satan was inevitable in witch superstition, as lycanthropy was one of the gifts. Now, certainly these ideas persisted longer in the Highlands. Wolves probably died out in the Lowlands by the thirteenth century, but they were still around in the Highlands in the eighteenth century. There people made potions of poppy, beladonna and datura to aid them to turn into animals.

People believed that they could spot anyone with werewolf potential. Superstitious nonsense pointed towards extreme hairiness, straight eyebrows meeting over the nose, strong and claw-like fingers, small flat ears, and third finger on each hand being as long as the second . . . all these were characteristic signs of a werewolf.

It was thought possible to kill a werewolf (but only with a silver bullet) and at the point of death it was said they turned back into human form. From this idea stemmed all the stories of hunters wounding wolves, to learn later that some local person had suffered an injury to the same part of the anatomy.

Many an old Scots saying contained a wolf reference . . . when the sun shone during rain it was called 'a wolf's wedding' and when there were woolly clouds the old folk said 'today like sheep, tomorrow wolves'. Anyone able to obtain a wolf's tongue had an important medical amulet: boiled, it healed thorn gashes while a pierced wolf's tooth was the luckiest of all amulets.

As a symbol of sovereignty and nobility, the **lion** has a long history in the world's superstitious lore and a special place in Scottish mysticism. The lion as an emblem of Scottishness probably began to achieve national favour in the reign of William the Lion (1165–1214), himself called the 'Friend of God and the Lion of Justice'; although before it became associated with Scottish royalty, the lion had been used on the banners of such as Alan, Lord of Galloway – thus the Lion of Galloway was a special protector of the west lands – and the Earls of Northumberland. The heraldry expert Alexander Nisbet averred that Scots in the army of Charlemagne, the Holy Roman Emperor, were carrying lion banners into battle as early as AD 800.

The first Scottish King to use the lion rampant on his seal was William the Lion's son, Alexander II (1214–49). Yet it was Alexander III (1249–86) who displayed the full design of the red lion rampant on the Scottish Royal Arms. So from the thirteenth century the lion was a 'Scottish beast' and appeared as a symbol of Scotland on the seal of the Guardians of Scotland.

The famous Scottish poet William Dunbar (c.1460–1520) summed up for all the significance of Scottish mystic lore about the lion:

'This awful beast was terrible of cheir,
Piercing of look and stout of countenance,
Right strong of corps in fashion fair but fier,
Lusty of shape, light of deliverance;
Red of his colour as the ruby glance,
On field of gold he stood full mightily,
With fleur-de-lis circled pleasantly'.

Hallowed Trees and Mystic Plants

MANOR churchyard lies some four miles from Peebles wherein was buried that curious little man of short stature called David Ritchie whom Sir Walter Scott immortalised in *The Black Dwarf* as Elshender. Nature had played a cruel trick on David: his torso was broad and of normal size, his arms were as powerful as any Border blacksmith, but his head was big and his expression was full of ugly malevolence, and his legs were really no more than twisted stumps. In his youth he had borne the jeers and scorn of Edinburgh folk as he endeavoured to earn his living as a brush-maker. At last their stares and taunts drove him back to the seclusion of Peeblesshire and the quiet of the Manor valley where, on land belonging to the farm of Woodhouse, he built himself a cottage. And there in 1796 or 1797 he was visited by Sir Walter Scott, a frequent guest at nearby Hallyards where the Ferguson family lived. The cottage we see today, though, was the one built for David in 1802 by Sir James Nasmyth of Posso.

The little man's knowledge of trees and plants was phenomenal and he knew all the Border superstitions concerning trees and flowers. Himself an inspired gardener, Ritchie's plots reflected the mystic powers he believed the plants had with his beds of **daffodils** to bring him more gold than silver and **mimosa** to charm away the Evil Eye. Just before he died 'Bowed Davie', as he was called, said that he must have a **rowan** (mountain ash) planted near his grave to keep witches away: and so it was done when he died in 1811 but alas, although the gravestone of 1845, erected by W and R Chambers, is still there, David Ritchie's unusual physique proved too much of a temptation to later resurrectionists.

David Ritchie's obsession with ash trees recalled the Norse myth long known in Scotland which told how man was created from the wood of the ash – *yggdrasil*, 'Tree of the World' which binds together heaven, earth and hell – by the god Odin, hero of the warriors. The wood of the rowan had been used by the Vikings to build their ships, to protect them against Ran, enemy of seamen. Also, in David Ritchie's day, Border folk often used rowan timber for the crossbeams of their chimneys, or for making water-mills or farm implements.

The ash was deemed anathema to snakes; and to sport an ash twig in the hat protected the wearer against snake bite. Witches, as David Ritchie would have told you, kept a safe distance from ash trees and a bunch of ash keys – the winged seeds of the tree – was once suspended by the fireplace in Border homes to keep the hell-dames away. Ash sap was fed to the newborn and a baby's first bath would be before a fire of ash wood for luck. A bunch of ash leaves protected bed and sleeping occupant from evildoers and often ash logs were burned to keep the Devil away, as was the original Yule log. As ash could not injure animals it was said, shepherds from Buchan to the Borders made their crooks from the wood.

The **hazel**, too, was thought efficacious against witchcraft, and Scots kept double hazel-nut clusters to protect them against the evils of necromancy when the spirits of the dead were incited by the evil to wreak havoc in a parish. Children born in Autumn were often given the 'milk' from hazel-nuts as their first food as it brought health and good luck; hazel milk mixed with honey was long used by Scots country folk as a tonic for lethargic children. It is still remembered as a Highland tradition that hazel was one of the Nine Sacred Woods needed to kindle the need-fire at Beltane. The word 'calton' (Gaelic *calltuinn*) for hazel perpetuates the local sacred groves of these trees at Edinburgh and Glasgow.

Once almost every Scottish parish had its own gallows from which to launch miscreants into eternity. Many a place-name recalls just where the gallows were – Hangman's Road at Cupar, Fife, is one example – but many a tree was shunned because of its purpose. Not long ago the popular press quoted a case in point, the story of the tree that used to stand by a dangerous corner of the road from Glenelg that follows the edge of the Sound of Sleat. The tree was a danger to the motorist, so it was cut down and split up for firewood and piled near the road so that locals could help themselves. But, no-one would touch the wood so strong was the superstition connected with it. The old tree had been the hanging tree for the Glenelg area, where horse-thieves, sheep stealers, robbers and murderers had danced out their penance suspended from its branches. In particular the older villagers would having nothing to do with it – they said it would bring bad luck to burn its logs. Some of the young folk scoffed and filled their wheelbarrows, but when they attempted to burn the logs their houses were filled with a peculiar smell – some said of decaying corpses. The firewood was returned and lay there to rot.

Another tree associated with death superstition was the **yew**, an old symbol of everlasting life and a power against death itself. To cut down a yew tree growing in a churchyard was deemed very unlucky, as was bringing yew branches into a house. The yew makes up part of the witches' potion in *Macbeth*:

'Gall of goat, and slips of yew
Sliver'd in the moon's eclipse.'

'Sliver'd' means that the yew branches had been broken in the wind and were doubly dangerous as they still contained the power of the storm that had torn them apart. In the days of clan warfare, a chief would hold a piece of churchyard yew in his left hand and threaten his enemies before the fight to enhance success. The superstition went that the enemy would not hear the denunciation and would thus be overcome by a surprise attack.

The **birch**, whose mystic potency was brought to Scotland by the Norsemen, was sacred to Thor, son of Odin, and was a symbol of Spring. If ever one should be planted in the policies of a house, it was a protective agent against the Evil Eye, lightning, gout and barrenness. And every vigilant housewife knew that a witch's broomstick was made of birch.

In the quadrangle of Queen Mary's College, South Street, St Andrews, Queen Mary's Thorn – the **hawthorn** whose ancestral rootstock was deemed to have been planted by Mary Queen of Scots around 1565 – and the Glastonbury Thorn which flowers during a mild Christmas and was planted by college students to commemorate Principal Duncan's term of office 1949–50 are reminders of the old Scots belief about the may tree or hawthorn. It was deemed unwise to sit under a hawthorn when fairy activity was expected, on May Day, Midsummer Eve, or Hallowe'en, for to do so courted being enchanted. But to shelter there during a thunderstorm was a protection against lightning.

Near to Queen Mary's Thorn stands a two-hundred-year-old holm oak, the **oak** being long venerated by the Norsemen and the Celts as the thunder tree, sacred of Thor. Often the Scots country folk boiled acorns to use in folk medicine as a cure for drunkenness.

The nuts of many trees, by the by, were long associated with love, marriage and childbirth, as symbols of life and fertility. Once Hallowe'en was known as Nutcrack Night when nuts were used for divination. The superstitious Scots girl of yesteryear, should she wish to divine whether or not her beloved was true to her, would place two hazel-nuts – one to represent herself and one her lover – and set them side by side at the family grate. If they burned away in unison, she had nothing to worry about. But, if they exploded and flew apart – or failed to burn – she knew that her love was being false to her.

The **apple** was regarded by Scotland's Celtic ancestors as the talisman which led people to the Lands of the Gods wherein the fruit was eaten as ambrosia. The felling of an apple tree was once a very unlucky act in Scotland, for the tree was a symbol of immortality and eternal youth.

Elder trees have also had a long tradition of magical and mythological association, and in Christian times pagan superstition was transferred to the tree deemed the one Judas Iscariot committed suicide on. In the old days few folk would burn elder for fear of encouraging the Devil to come down the chimney. Strike a man dead with an elder stick, said the old lore, and his hand will reach out of the grave for retribution; and, beat a child with an elder and he or she will stop growing. Make a boat of elder and you will surely sink, said others, and make a child's cradle from elder and the infant would be prey to fairies.

There was indeed hardly a tree in Scotland that did not have its own superstitious lore. Lightning would never strike an **elm** tree as it was sacred to the Cheviot elves they said in Roxburghshire; Christ's Cross was made of **aspen** said the devout of Peebles, so its leaves tremble in the breeze; but leaves of the **bay** placed under the pillow, added the folk of Selkirkshire, would bring pleasant dreams. In southwest Scotland, long life was assured for a child should its toys be made of oak, but bad luck would fall on those who trod on **holly** berries. Where a **myrtle** grows, insisted Kirkcudbrightshire people, houses nearby would be filled with love and peace.

The subject of myriad Scottish legends and superstitions, many flowers and plants are considered unlucky if brought into the house, particularly those that are highly scented, or have drooping heads, or white blooms. To dream of white flowers is an old omen of death, while to take red and white flowers into a hospital was considered very bad luck for the same reason. **White heather** is one of the few exceptions, but white **lilac** was deemed the most potently evil flower for the house. To burn heather, by the by, was to bring on the rain.

An anti-witch plant, **clover**, was considered lucky to wear as a hat decoration or in the lapel, especially if it was of the very rare four-leafed variety. Clover gave the power of recognising evil spirits, whereas **cowslip**, another pastoral neighbour, when made into wine was a cure-all for a wide range of stubborn diseases.

Buttercups were thought to be a cure for insanity if tied around a sick person's neck; but the flower was a better cure for toothache if sprinkled with salt and hung from one finger. **Ferns** were widely used as folk medicine too against snake-bites, coughs, inflammation and sore eyes. But to cut them on a Sunday was courting bad luck; worse would befall, however, if you cut **foxgloves** on the Lord's Day.

The legends of the **corn** spirits have been particularly tenacious in Scotland and rural folk had a whole range of superstitions connected with the treatment of corn, from threshing and winnowing of the harvest to the brewing of ale. As a race memory from their pagan ancestors, Scots farmers who cut the last sheaf of the harvest invested in it the spirit of femininity. If it were cut before Hallowe'en the sheaf was called 'the Maiden', and if after Hallowe'en 'the Auld Wife' or *Cailleach* in the Highlands. In some areas of the Highlands it was dressed up as an old woman in cap and frock, apron and shawl, and carried to the farmhouse where it had pride of place at the head of the table. The sheaf was then put away after harvest until Christmas when it was given as fodder to a mare in foal, or a cow in calf. In some places the dressed sheaf was 'danced' at the harvest ball as a direct descendant of the Corn Mother of pagan Europe.

Ivy, the kindly plant of Christmas decoration or potion for jaundice, was used in southern Scotland for divination. A girl would put a leaf of ivy against her heart and recite:

'Ivy, ivy,I love you,
In my bosom I put you.
The first young man who speaks to me
My future husband he shall be.'

No look at superstitions about Scottish flora would be complete without a mention of the mystic three, the **bluebells**, **gowans** and **thistles**. Known as the harebell in Scottish folklore, the bluebell has always been a lucky symbol and was used as an amulet if a rare white one was found. The gowan, or daisy, was the plant picked and kept close by those who suffered from eye complaints. Even so it was the flower of melancholy, the red blood of its leaves remembering the martyrdom of St John the Baptist, upon whose feast, 27 August, gowans were displayed in churches in medieval Scotland. Used in love divination with the jingle 'He (or she) loves me, he loves me not', the plucked petals of the gowan denoted the truth of love in its remaining petal.

'The rough bur thistle spreading wide,
Among the bearded bear,
I turned the weeder chips aside,
And spared the symbol dear.'

Thus wrote Robert Burns of the thistle, a mystic symbol of Scotland's nationhood that was very old in his time. Apocryphal though it may be, legend has it that a Scots army were encamped near modern Kingskettle in Fife, when an army of marauding Danes approached the slumbering camp. One of the Danes trod on a thistle and let out a yell that aroused the Scots who vanquished the enemy and hailed the thistle as their saviour. In truth the thistle head did not make its appearance as a Scottish emblem until the minting of the groats of James III in 1471. Today this luck device symbolises the Scots' underlying character, tough and tetchy.

Superstitions of the Living and the Dead

WHY was it that your parents were so concerned to choose an appropriate **name** for you at the time of your birth? Your mother and father sensed the old beliefs which laid down that a name must reflect the particular character you were destined by birth to reflect. In northern Europe a name was considered magical, for its sound would be spelled out in the runes, those mystical picture letters which could keep evil forces from the living and the dead.

Sometimes a child's name was kept secret until its baptism, to keep it free from witchcraft.

Old Scottish beliefs and customs concerning **childbirth** lingered long as a legacy of the time when birth was a dangerous trauma and a mystery. Before the modern maternity hospitals, births in castle and cottage alike were supervised by 'auld spey wifies', who attended layings out and layings in with equal gusto. This competent old woman made sure that all the doors were unlocked and all knots loosened to ease the passage of birth; the same ritual was gone through to ease death. It was widely believed that malevolent persons hindered birth by tying knots before and during a woman's labour. In poorer houses women were lifted unto the earth floor of the kitchen so that they might draw strength from the earth in the last stages of travail. Nails were hammered into the bedposts to keep away demons and bad fairies.

It was believed, too, that the pain of giving birth could be shared by, or transferred to, a husband by placing the man's clothes over the woman at the moment of her delivery. The same result, of course, could be done by spells. Thomas Pennant (1726–98), the famous naturalist and traveller who toured Scotland, wrote *Tours in Scotland* (1771–95) and of whom Dr Samuel Johnson said 'he observes more things than anyone else does' noted at Langhom, Dumfries, in

1772 that 'the midwives had the power of transfer-
ring part of the primeval curse bestowed upon our
first great mother from the good wife to her husband. I saw the reputed offspring of such a labour,
who kindly came into the world without giving the
mother the least uneasiness, whilst the poor husband
was roaring with agony and in foul and unnatural
pains'.

When the birth process was over mother and child
were often introduced to the 'household deities' through
the practice of 'saining' (Blessing). A fir candle was lit and
carried three times around the birth chamber. Then a
Bible and a crumb or two of bread was placed under
the mother's pillow with the words: 'May the Almighty
debar a' ill frae this wumman, an' be aboot her, an' bless
her an' her bairn'.

Alternatively, the child itself would be carried round
the room twice and placed next to the ingle nook 'the
abode of the little people'. An extension of this was that
a woman was not allowed to enter any other house until
she had been churched . . . purified of the evil spirits
which emanated from the rigors of birth . . . so that
such evil would not be transferred to someone else's
dwelling.

Because of Celtic influence, stories of **changelings**
are legion in Scotland — the birth of a weak, dark and
undernourished infant was considered to be a fairy
child. If such a child be born it would be placed near
the fire; and were it really a changeling it would after
a while, fly 'up the lum' (chimney). The most famous
changeling story was that attached to James Stuart,
who grew up to be King James VI of Scotland and
I of England. He had been born at Edinburgh Castle
on 19 June 1566, the son of Mary, Queen of Scots,
and Henry Stewart, Lord Darnley. The discovery of
some nameless bones of a child at the castle in the
mid 1800's gave rise to the far-fetched tale that James
Stuart had died at birth and a dark fairy baby had been
substituted; indeed gossips said it was a child of the Earl
of Mar.

James's birth, incidentally, was also connected with
another superstition that was associated with **cauls**, for

called Regulus brought relics of St Andrew to Scotland. The story goes that Regulus was warned in a dream that the bones of Andrew were to be removed from Patras to Constantinople by Emperor Constantine II. So an angel directed Regulus to take relics of Andrew – three finger bones, an arm bone and a knee cap – and carry them to safety to 'the uttermost end of the earth'. All this happened around AD 340, and Regulus is said to have landed at Muckross, afterwards Kilrymont (modern St Andrews), where he founded a church.

There are other versions of the myths about Regulus and St Andrew, but we can be sure that the cult of St Andrew was established in Scotland by the eighth century, and Andrew, with his decussate cross became the 'spirit of Scotland'. The saint and his cross was thereafter to be used as a sacred and superstitious symbol of Scottish nationhood and power.

This symbolism was used on a wide range of medieval artifacts from the seals of the Bishops of St Andrews diocese and the 1418 mace of the Faculty of Arts of the university of St Andrews, to the company badges of such regiments as the Scots Guards with the words *In hoc signo vinces* (In this sign thou shalt conquer). For armies to see the sign of the cross in the sky was deemed to be a signal of victory to come.

Incidentally, St Andrew on his cross appeared on the seal of the Guardians of Scotland (1286–92) surrounded by the motto *Andrea Scotis Dux est et compatriotis* (Andrew is the leader of the Scots and compatriots): and it was on the saint's day (30 November) that John Baliol was crowned in 1292. After he was deposed the English balladists sang that now the Scots must be companions of the Devil, for Andrew had not saved them.

From belfries of abbeys, churches and cathedrals from Arbroath to Jedburgh **bells** tolled the passage of life and death in medieval Scotland, in that long tradition of the ritual, magic and social uses of bells from time immemorial. Once the bells of Scotland were given saints' names to help them sound, the superstitious said, and combat the evil spirits of earth and air who brought storms and accidents. In the presence of a bishop, or his deputy, Scotland's bells were washed with water, anointed with oil and salt and crossed in the name of the Holy Trinity for potency, and new bells were processed on their flower-strewn way to the belfry.

The bells were often inscribed with such mottoes as 'I call the quick to church and dead to grave' and the healing power of bells was an old superstition in Scotland. They were rung in time of plague to disperse 'the corrupte aires' and often in Scotland the head of a corpse was pillowed on a handbell as an additional insurance against the Devil's machinations before burial.

Scots superstition has always reflected the idea that **death** was a difficult process. So, as with birth, certain customs and rituals were practised to give the dead an 'easy passing'. Thus all the locks in a house should be opened, bolts should be withdrawn and knots loosened to help the souls depart. It was important to make sure that the dying person's head was not resting on a pigeon or dove feather pillow, as this would inhibit dying. Sometimes a dying person was lifted out of bed and onto the ground – the earth, from which mankind springs 'earth to earth, ashes to ashes', would help the journey.

In the Scottish Lowlands there was a curious superstitious salt-rite, called *dishaloof*, enacted after a death. When the cadaver had been laid out, the oldest woman in the room waved a lighted candle three times over the body and laid three handfuls of salt on the breast. Then three empty dishes, with a sieve between them, were set near the fire; the underlying idea being that the soul of a dead person hovers near to the fireplace for a set time after death. All present in the room then went out and returned backwards, reciting what was known as the Saining Rhyme. With their backs still turned, they tried to put their hands into the sieve. The first to do so was thought to have released the soul from its earthly bondage; but if no one managed to do this, the soul was deemed to be earthbound for some time.

Scots long observed that death of living creatures involved the ceasing of the flow of **blood** and that when a man was wounded and lost blood, he weakened and expired. Thus the belief arose that a creature's blood was its life force and because of this powerful magic liquid, blood entered Scottish superstitious lore.

It is an old belief in Scotland that blood itself cries out for vengeance in a murdered person. For many years they tried to scrub the blood from a floor in a room in Glamis castle where Macbeth was deemed to have murdered King Duncan; they failed, the bloodstain refused to go and the floor was boarded over. Such indelible blood forced the cry from the tormented lips of Lady Macbeth: 'Out, damned spot! Out, I say'. And so because of the belief, suspected murderers in Scotland were once forced to touch a corpse of their victim to see if indictment would come through the cadaver bleeding afresh. Sir Walter Scott remembered this in his old ballad of Earl Richard:

'The maiden touched the clay cauld corpse
A drap of it never bled.
A layde laid her hand on him
And soon the ground was red.'

Where blood fell, the old folk said, grass would never grow, and a witch could be neutralised by causing her blood to drip – 'Scoring above the breath' was the old ritual of scratching charms associated with blood. In her *Highland Chapbook* (1928), Isabel Cameron tells us of the highland charm to stop a haemorrhage. You said this in a loud voice over the wounded person:

'The charm of God is great:
The free gift of Mary:
The free gift of God:
The free gift of every Priest and Churchman:
The free gift of Michael the Strong:
That would put strength into the sun.'

Thus the old pagan idea mixed with Christian prayer.

Nose-bleeds have a curious superstitious lore in Scotland. To be taken with a sudden attack of epistaxis was a sign of impending misfortune; but if it happened in the presence of a certain person a love element was indicated. Blood from both nostrils forecast a family death, while one flow from a right hand nostril meant family fortune.

Sealing agreements by the ritual signing in one's own blood was known as the Blood Covenant. In credence of the old custom some of the signatories of the Scottish National Covenant of 1638 in Greyfriars Churchyard, Edinburgh, did so in their own blood.

The **candles** on a birthday cake remind us of the time when the light from a candle represented a person's individual existence in the mortal world. But in Scotland most of the lore concerning candles is associated with the dead.

A guttering candle in castle or bothy foretold of a life nearing its end; and should a candle burn with a dim blue flame a spirit was passing. A wavy flame though, in a place where there was no draught indicated bad weather to come, and it was unlucky to leave a candle burning in an empty room as it encouraged death itself to creep up.

In the Highland's on St Bridget's Eve (31 January) a bed was placed near the door of a house and one of the family went outside and shouted: 'Bridget, Bridget, come in, thy bed is ready'. One or two candles were placed by the bed to burn through the night. The rite was to encourage Irish St Bridget of Kildare (the Scottish equivalent of the Roman Brigantia) patroness of craftsmen and fertility, bringer of the Spring, to hasten to dispel the dark and cold of winter. The Feast of Bridget (1 February) corresponded with the old Celtic fertility feast of *Imbolc*.

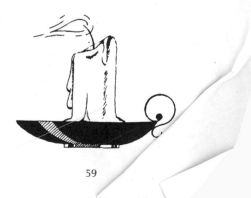

Nuns are Luckier than Monkey Puzzle Trees

MOST children still share that awe which Mole felt in the Edinburgh-born author Kenneth Grahame's book *The Wind in the Willows*. Ratty warned Mole about the dozens of things an animal had first to learn before he went into the Wild Wood: 'Passwords, and signs, and sayings which have power and effect, and plants you carry in your pocket, and verses you repeat, and dodges and tricks you practise; all simple enough when you know them, but they've got to be known if you're small, or you'll get yourself into trouble.'

Thus children warned each other that it was unlucky to cry on your **birthday**. It was also important to blow out all the candles on your birthday cake at once or your special wish would not come true. In days past a birthday boy or girl had their hair pulled once for every year.

Never wear a **new coat** with pockets, unless you've put something in, another superstition warned. A cardigan put on the wrong way round by mistake must be worn that way for the rest of the day for good luck.

'Touch your hair, touch your toes
And hope you'll never be in one of those.'

Was the rhyme Scots children chanted when they saw an **ambulance**, while at Ballingry and Cowdenbeath, Fife, children recited 'It's no ma Dye, an' it's no ma Grannie' when they saw a large black **slug** or **snail**; the chant was followed by a spit on the poor beast.

Most children's superstitions are connected with things outside, whether people met, objects found ˅ chance, or mascots carried for good luck. Some 'dren warn each other that it is unlucky to speak a walking under a **railway bridge**. To walk under beʳ was to ensure that you got the strap that day the Highland children remembered, on the day of ⁺ion, the Devil, in mortal guise, stood directˡ

60

underneath the ladder, while the Roman soldiers took
down the bodies. So to walk under a ladder at all was
dire bad luck. You also, of course, broke the mystic
'Angle of Fate' by walking under a ladder for you split
the angle made by the ladder, the wall and the ground.
In Aberdeen, though, where the act of spitting is added
to many superstitions, to spit after you walked under a
ladder would reverse the bad luck.

'To catch a **leaf** as it falls from a tree gives a wish
or a day's good luck', other children reasoned. But in
Aberdeen it was a **mail van** that brought the best luck.
It was lucky to see a Royal Mail Van; and to set the good
luck going you had to touch wood. Should a group of
children see a mail van pass they would shout 'First for
the Royal Mail Van', 'Second for the Royal Mail Van'
and so on until the van had come to a stop. Then the
children ran to touch the gold crown on its side in the
order of shouting which would bring good luck according to the old rhyme also linked with **sneezing**:

> 'One's a wish,
> Two's a kiss,
> Three's a disappointment,
> Four's a letter,
> Five is better,
> Six is best of all.'

Nuns were deemed luckier than **monkey-puzzle trees**.
Edinburgh children knew that to see three nuns walking
together was a good luck sign; but the reverse was true if
you saw three monkey-puzzle trees in the same day.

To point at a **rainbow** is generally believed to be
unlucky, for it will bring rain, but in Ballingry, Fife,
children said that the first to see a rainbow would be
the luckiest in the village that day, especially if the person said 'I'm first to see the rainbow'. Some of these
old superstitions were transferred to more modern artifacts. One boy remembered that in his home village at
Cowdenbeath the rainbow superstition was applied to
the new electric street lamps which were set up in the
1930s.

hair will

Step on the **cracks** of a pavement *was more*
out they said at Lanark; but in

dire as it was prophesied that you would fall downstairs.
To walk on these cracks you 'break the Devil's dishes'
they said in Buchan.

Finding buttons, coins, bits of coal, rings and sticks
with a fork in the wood were all lucky things to find in
the street; but the **horseshoe** was luckiest of all. 'When
you see a horseshoe lying on the ground, pick it up, spit
on it and throw it over your shoulder' the children of
Angus were advised. For this reason **pins** – particularly
bent ones – were lucky to find:

'See a pin and pick it up
All the day you'll hae guid luck
See a pin and let it lay
Ill luck you'll have all that day.'

Something **silver** in the pocket, or a piece of **coal**,
would bring good luck in school examinations. Mascots of all kinds too, from dolls to favourite toys, have
all been petitioned for success in games, but **crossed
fingers** are the best luck action of all for courage.

Of all the superstitious rituals for finding a sweetheart's
name, children have favoured the **plum** or **cherry** stone
routines best of all. What you did was, when you had
prunes or cherries for dinner, you would range them
round your plate and count out 'Tinker, tailor, soldier,
sailor, rich man, poor man, beggar man, thief'; which-
ever name you stopped at would be your sweetheart,
said the girls, from Fort William to Forfar. Indeed in
Forfar the girls further counted out: 'Silk, satin, muslin
or rags' and then 'big house, small house, pigsty or
barn', to find out what they would be married in and
where they would live.

Children have always found **warts** an embarrass-
ment and several superstitious cures were invented.
Everything from egg yolk to ink was prescribed as a
miraculous unguent. The wart touched with a small
thief elderberry would be sure to go if dismissed with
ne:

W
Ple t, on my knee
way, one two three.'

The twig had then to be thrown into flowing water.

Freckles on the other hand were given a better superstitious lore, they were thought to be a sign of a happy nature. While **dimples** showed the way to destiny:

'A dimple in your chin
Your fortune will come in
A dimple on your cheek
Your fortune's far to seek.'

The Secret World of Elfame

OF ALL the spirit creatures who have inhabited Scottish folkfore since time began, the denizens of Elfame are the most prominent. These **fairy folk**, in their own kingdom that lies parallel with our time and space, can be easily distinguished from other spirits such as **brownies**, **elves** and **gnomes**. Or so the old folk said. By tradition fairies are beautiful folk in human form. More angelic perhaps than mortals the fairies were distinguished also by their dress of bright green.

Their origins are ascribed to Celtic myth, and they dwelt long in the minds of mankind in the Highlands and Islands of Scotland in particular. They were usually described as *daoine-sith*, 'good neighbours', but if slighted they could be cruel and spiteful and bore grudges for centuries. One fault all fairies possessed, of course, was that they readily kidnapped human unbaptised children and adults, particularly young married females, to become nurses to the fairy children.

People once took 'fairy grudges' seriously and many remember the story connected with Langton House, some two miles southwest of Duns, Berwickshire. Many centuries ago the fairies had a grudge against the Coburn family of Langton and, as a punishment, threatened to take the house away to Dogton Moss, some miles away near to Greenlaw village. One moonlit night, then, the fairies gathered at Langton and began to loosen the house's foundations. Singing as they worked, the fairies were just about to lift the house when one of the Coburns woke up. Terrified by the house's movement, as in a terrible earthquake, he rushed to the window to see the fairies about their vengeful work. ening one of the sash windows the man shouted h top of his voice: 'O Lord keep me and the pogether.' His prayer, it seems, broke the fairies' safe little creatures fled and the house remaine the undations until it was legally demolished

The Scottish fairies lived underground, or in little green tumuli, called *sitheanan* in Gaelic, wherein the royal fairies held their courts amid a splendour of artifacts. Some stories even fix the Fairy Court at Tom-na-hurich, the Hill of the Yews, above Inverness. Those with the eyes to see them, could watch their pageants and processions in the green wood that were more magnificent than any Eastern potentate. The fairies rode on milk-white steeds and wore dresses brilliant beyond belief and danced to a music that no human hand or voice could produce.

Some even said that the skilled bagpipers, the MacCrimmons of Skye and the MacArthurs of Pein-gowen, had fairy friends who supplied them with special reeds and pipes to enhance their musical powers. Some half a mile from the Roxburghshire village of Ednam, they still point out the knoll known as the Piper's Grave. In reality a Pictish burial mound, local legend dubbed it a fairy hill into which once sneaked a local piper eager to learn the music secrets of the little folk. As he entered without a protective talisman he vanished never to be seen again.

One man who knew the fairies well was Sir Thomas Learmont, known to literature as Thomas the Rhymer of Erceldoune. He lived around 1220–97 and inherited lands in the Berwickshire village of Earlston, where his tower can still be seen. A man who could see clearly into the future, Thomas is deemed to have forecast the death of Alexander III – who perished in 1286, when his horse stumbled over the cliff near Pettycur Bay, Fife – and the battle of Bannockburn of 1314.

The old superstitious tales tell us that Thomas the Rhymer received his prophetic powers from the **Queen of Elfame** herself, when he became ensnared by her magic. He met her, the tales recounted, on the slope of the Eildon Hills, Roxburghshire:

'True Thomas lay on Huntly bank,
A ferlie spied he with his e'e;
For there he saw a layde bright
Come riding down by Eildon tr

> Her shirt was o' the grass-green silk,
> Her mantle o' the velvet fyne;
> At ilka telt o' her horse's mane   *every braid*
> Hung fifty siller bells and nine.

The vision of the queen which came down to the superstitious was that her steed was of ivory, inlaid with gold, she had a quiver of arrows on her back and a bow in one hand; and with the other she led three hounds on a leash.

So for many the Fairy Kingdom in Scotland was somewhere in the side of Eildon Hill, which lies a mile or so south of Melrose. Indeed the Eildons protect a fairy secret which is famous in Scotland's lore, for in the depths of the hill, legend says, King Arthur and his knights lie sleeping to await recall by fairy horn to do battle with Britain's enemies.

A man who was deemed to have encountered the king was Richard the horse-dealer from Canonbie, Dumfriesshire. Known as Canonbie Dick he was riding home from market one evening with two horses he had been unable to sell at the Melrose fair. As he rode along he was stopped by a man in strangely antique clothing who asked to buy the horses. After some argy-bargy about price they settled a deal and Dick was paid in gold pieces of long passed denomination. To seal the bargain Dick was invited back to the man's home for a drink, with the warning that if Dick lost his nerve when he saw where the man lived he would vanish from the face of the earth.

Dick silently scoffed at the warning and followed the man to the place called Lucken Hare, where the man entered into Eildon hillside through a concealed door. Astonished, Dick found himself in a huge cavern down the walls of which were rows of sleeping knights sitting ʌtride their horses. On a table lay a sword and a horn, ₅the man offered Dick the choice of drawing the fir or blowing the horn. If he chose the correct one tim` he, Dick, would be King of Scotland for aˡ it. Aˡ chose the horn and endeavoured to blᴄ up in ˟ the wrong choice and a huge wind bˡ n and blew Dick out of the hill. As cˣ broke Dick was found by shepherds at the foot of Eildon Hill; he told them his story and then expired.

The most precious treasure owned by the MacLeods of Skye is the *Bratach Sith*, the '**Fairy Flag**' which hangs in Dunvegan Castle. Should the MacLeods be in peril, the old story goes, all they have to do is wave the flag. The fairy magic, it appears, only works three times and the MacLeods have already unfurled it twice in battle at Glendale in 1490 and Waternish in 1520; each time they were saved from annihilation by the MacDonalds. Experts say that the faded brown silk flag probably came from Syria or Rhodes, but legend gives other sources.

One story recounts how the MacLeods acquired it from a fairy woman sometime in the fourteenth century. She had been married to the clan chief for twenty years and on her return to Elfame she gave him the flag as a gift; the place of their parting is still pointed out as the Fairy Bridge near the castle. Another story avers that the flag is the banner called Land-Ravager which was carried into battle by the Norse King Harald Hardrada who perished at Britain's other Battle of 1066 at Stamford Bridge.

Should you by chance encounter fairy soldiers you would recognise them by the fairy flags. Although they were used much earlier, we can be sure that the mystic significance of flags was established by the reign of King William the Lion (1165-1214), whose soldiers carried the *breachbennach* (speckled banner) before them in the hands of a monk from Arbroath Abbey.

Another beast from the land of Elfame used on Scottish flags was the **dragon**. A banner with this beast was carried before David I at the Battle of the Standard (1138).

Those anxious to see **fairy soldiers** are advised by the folk who know about these things to journey to the woods about the Cloanaig stream at Loch Fyne, Argyll. There, south of Skipness, from time to time the fairy army is seen dressed in green livery.

Several of the wretched creatures arraigned for witchcraft in Scotland professed to be in cahoots with the fairies. One such was Alison Pearson who averred that she received her skills as a herbalist directly from the fairies. One of her customers was Patrick Adamson, Archbishop of St Andrews, who took medicine prescribed by her. In deference to the old superstition he is said to have taken the medicine so that the illness from which he suffered would be transferred to his horse. Alison Pearson had played a dangerous game and was tried at Byrehill in 1588 and was found guilty of witchcraft and consigned to the flames.

Despite the Borderers' devotion to the fairies, undoubtedly the most active of the Scottish fairies were the *sithiche*, the fairy sprites of Highland folklore. They were skilled child-stealers so all sorts of rituals were enacted in the highlands to protect children from their machinations; a popular act was to dress a child in red ribbons for security.

If slighted the fairies might go so far as killing mortals with their stone arrows tipped with yellow known as *saighdean sithe* ('fairy arrows'). Not even the dead were beyond the reach of fairies. In the parish of Lunan, Angus, it was once the practice to burn the chaff and bedstraw on which a dying body had lain on the nearest fairy tumulus to make sure that the fairies did not interfere with the spirit of the dead person.

Keep on the right side of fairies and they will reward you, the old folk said, and there is many a Scottish story to prove their point. As he passed Rubers Law, near Hawick, one old shepherd came across a fairy woman who was lamenting that she had nothing to wrap her baby in to keep it warm. The shepherd gave her his own plaid from his shoulders and went on his way. At the next fair he found that his sheep sold at the highest prices ever and that his fortune was made; prices of course elevated by fairy influence!

It was the brownies and the elves who undertook the work in Elfame, said the believers, and from time to time they work for mortals. In the annals of Claypots Castle, at Broughty Ferry, Angus, there is the story of the industrious brownie who did all the work at the castle in exchange for a daily bowl of cream. The brownie left because he could not bear to watch indolent servants. One kitchen girl annoyed him with her slovenliness and he beat her with kale stems. So wrathful was he that he cursed the castle and left for ever.

They will tell you at Glenlivet, in Banffshire, that the last brownie left the area in the 1870s. Called locally, 'an old household goblin' the brownie had the mortal name of Maggie Moloch (or Hairy Meg to the less kind) and she lived at the farm of Achnarrow. Sometimes she went around the countryside with a brownie called Clod.

Maggie Moloch, it appears, milked the cows and did household chores and like the brownie of Claypots she was fed with cream and a daily oatcake. The farm fell on bad times in the 1870s and the farmer had to sack his workers. Maggie was enraged and tipped all the milk away after the cows had been milked and refused to do household chores. Rather than annoy Maggie more the farmer reinstated the workers and Maggie was mollified to continue her work until one day she vanished.

Perhaps the most curious piece of superstitious fairy lore in Scotland is that about the Isle of Eynhallow – or Holy Isle after its twelfth-century monastery – Orkney's most romantic island. Uninhabited today, folk legend has the spellbound island as once belonging to the fairies, who were able to make it vanish from time to time.

The Devil and All His Works

IF THE Scots do not exactly love the Devil, they treat him with great respect. No other character in Scottish superstitious lore has so many **nicknames** than the Devil: Auld Clootie, Nickie-ben, Auld Hornie, The Guidman, Auld Sandie, Auld Chiel, Auld Harry, and the Earl of Hell are but a few. In all there are twenty-nine nicknames identified and the most unusual is Auld Waghorn; now Waghorn was a fabulous personage said to be a greater liar than the Devil himself and therefore King of Liars, and as many did not like to use the Devil's actual name – in case it brought them bad luck – they used the word Waghorn to describe him, or one of the other nicknames.

The Devil's name was also given to dozens of **place names** in Scotland. The chimney of his house (Hell's Lum) is set at Pennan, a fishing village in North Aberdeenshire. His staircase is situated near Glenluce, southeast of Stranraer, and his Mill is not far from Dollar at Rumbling Bridge, while his Cauldron is found at Comrie. As the Devil is larger than life, gargantuan artifacts were attributed to him. Again massive outcrops, curious natural features, eccentric architecture and anything with a sinister side to it were attributed to the Devil.

There is many a Scot too who admitted to meeting the Devil. John Knox hinted in his book *The Royal House of Stuart* that he had a conversation with the Devil in the cathedral churchyard at St Andrews. Again the famous Member of Parliament and compiler of statistics about Scotland, Sir John Sinclair, noted that Patrick Forbes, Bishop of Aberdeen, was abducted from his castle at Craigievar by the Devil who left his footprint in the gable end of the castle.

Even **proverbs** underlined the world of devilry:

'The Deil dances in an empty pocket.
There's a deil in every mouthful of whisky.

The Deil is busy in a high wind.
The Deil's guid tae his ain.
He needs a lang-shankit spuin that sups wi' the Deil.'

Many a mischievous little boy has been called 'a deil's buckie' as well.

One man above all others drew together the non-sense of the **superstitions** about the Devil in Scotland and made Auld Hornie into a marvellous character for satire. That man was Robert Burns in such poems as *Address to the Deil, Tam o'Shanter*, and *Epistle to Colonel de Peyster*. Through the figure of the Devil, Burns was the voice of humanity as he saw it, the voice of sane, humorous, unpretentious mankind. He took the Devil of the Church of Scotland's Calvinism and humanised him, reducing him to a figure of fun who was found to live in Hell's Kitchen. By doing so Burns attacked the Scots fear of the Devil which was used by the Scottish Kirk of his day to repress, threaten and terrify. All the things that the Scots minis-ters accredited to the Devil – dancing, drinking, loving and letting down the hair – Burns wrote up as gifts from the Devil.

While it was the witches of Scotland who were the most castigated for being in cahoots with the Devil, Satan was given a number of curious roles himself. He was, for instance, considered to be the master of chess playing and would use his skills to win souls. One such was the soul of King Robert II's rapacious son Alexander Stewart who lived at Ruthven Castle, near Kingussie, and was given the name of the 'Wolf of Badenoch'. On being excommunicated for not giving up his mistress, Alexander Stewart, Earl of Buchan and Ross, burned down Elgin cathedral. Soon folklore began to reflect his doings and averred that with his band of maurauders he practised witchcraft by night and pillaged the north of Scotland by day. Then, one stormy night, people from Kingussie observed a black-clad stranger ride up to Ruthven Castle. As they peered through the cas-tle windows they saw the stranger playing chess with Alexander. They watched the dark stranger move a piece on the board and shout 'Check'. As the echo died away the room was plunged into darkness and then lit by an unnatural ball of fire which consumed the room. The villagers fled. In the morning when the bravest of them returned they found the cadaver of Alexander and his henchmen within the blackened ruins of the castle. To this day local folk say that the Devil can be seen playing chess for the soul of Alexander Stewart in the ruins of the castle.

Needless to say, the Devil was a master of disguises and the unwary were warned by the superstitious to watch out for his incarnations, for he could turn himself into almost anything. One example of this comes from the folklore of the Covenanters.

The Covenanters, by the by, were a group of fanatical Puritan fundamentalists who saw themselves as the Lord's Chosen People. The name was given to the signatories of the Scottish National Covenant in 1638 who were pledged to uphold the Presbyterian faith against prelacy and popery. The Covenanters refused to sign the Oath of Allegiance after the Restoration of 1660. Now, two of their number David Dun and Halbert Dobson lived in the region of the Moffat Water, Dumfriesshire and they were on the run from Royalist troops. They hid themselves in a cliff face near to a waterfall called Dob's Linn.

Local legend has it that the Devil found out where they were hiding and tried a number of **disguises** to tempt the two men to break cover. The Devil was unable to do this and in return the two Covenanters made a number of crosses out of red thread and twigs to drive the Devil away. They then lay in wait for the Devil to make another sally at their position. Each armed with a Bible and a cross of rowan and red thread the Covenanters managed to topple the Devil down a cliff face when he made his appearance. The Devil fell down the waterfall, but saved himself from drowning by turning himself into a bundle of sheepskins which floated to safety.

Feats of great **strength** were nothing to the Devil the old folk said. He was able to hurl huge masses of rock at anything he did not like. Those who lived at Kirkton of Largo, Fife, said that Largo Law was a rock dropped by the Devil on his way across the county; and at the top of Largo Law is a formation still known as the Devil's Chair.

At the gateway of Crail's Auld Kirk, in the East Neuk of Fife, stands the Blue Boulder that legend says the Devil threw in a fit of anger from the Isle of May. He had intended to destroy the Church that was being built at the time and missed. It is said that as it flew through the air the boulder split, one part to land by the church gate and the other on nearby Balcomie beach. For many decades locals would point out the Devil's thumbprint on the stone by the kirk gate. There is a similar story connected with Dargie Church, Angus, where another large stone is pointed out as a missile of the Devil.

So important was the Devil in Scottish superstition then, that it is not surprising that today there is still a Scottish festival extant in which the Devil appears. 'St Ronan's Cleikum Ceremony' is part of the 'St Ronan's Border Games' which takes place during the third week of July at Innerleithen, a small Peeblesshire town on the Tweed.

Innerleithen was once a popular spa to which the sick and the hypochondriac came to benefit from the saline waters at the Well of St Ronan. Undoubtedly the watering place was given an enormous boost with the publication of Sir Walter Scott's novel *St Ronan's Well* in 1823.

Among the celebrated visitors to Innerleithen's spa in the mid-1820s were several members of the 'Edinburgh Six-Feet Club', which consisted of forty middle-class and upper-class men who were all six foot tall and over. Under their influence St Ronan's Border Games were established. According to John Gibson Lockhart, Walter Scott's son-in-law and fallacious biographer, the management of the games was taken on by 'a club of Bowmen of the Border, arrayed in doublets and Lincoln green, with broad blue bonnets, and having the Ettrick Shepherd (*i.e., the poet James Hogg*) as Captain'. Initially the games took in archery, jumping, racing, wrestling, stone-throwing and hammer-throwing.

In 1901 the Cleikum Ceremony was introduced. The object of this was to underline the traditions of the saint whose name the spa has. St Ronan was a seventh-century monk who was obsessed with the Devil and 'his dark majesty's interference with the life of men'. The saint was long represented (heraldically on the Burgh Arms) as 'cleikin' the diel by the hint leg' (catching the Devil by the hind leg) with his crozier – and Walter Scott had this design hanging above the doorway of Meg Dod's 'Cleikum Inn' in his story *St Ronan's Well*.

The Cleikum Ceremony is usually preceded by the Installation of Innerleithen's Standard Bearer in the local common ridings. The Standard Bearer is the leader of the townspeople in the enactment by the old well. At the well a schoolboy, who takes the part of St Ronan with his retinue of 'monks', meets the official party and the Standard Bearer drinks the spa water to monitor its continuing efficacy. The party then processes around the town.

By tradition the Cleikum Ceremony takes place on the following evening at an indoor meeting place. The proceedings begin with the festal song:

'Rouse ye, men of old St Ronan's
 Gather in from hills and commons,
 Ready aye to hear the summons,
 On St Ronan's On!'

Accompanied by the monks, the year's St Ronan is invested with his medal of office and his pastoral staff known as the Cleikum Crozier. Traditionally St Ronan has a female assistant who is likewise invested at this time. In the presence of the Standard Bearer a tableau representing the 'cleikin' o' the diel' takes place. The culmination of the St Ronan's Border Games is a bonfire on which the Devil is burned.

Many a Scottish village set out a piece of its best land for the devil or 'gudeman' and called it 'Cloutie's Croft'; locals shunned the ground and it was left untilled and uncropped.

Jewels of Love and Magic

AFTER Queen Victoria popularised Scotland from the tourist angle, from her first visit to the country in 1842, there was a boom in jewellery manufacture with Scottish motifs, from grouse claws to cairngorm brooches.

The utilisation of 'Scotch pebbles', or agates, was old when the Victorians became interested, for they had long been used as amulets and talismans. An **amulet**, by the by, may be described as an object which is believed to have a beneficial influence on its owner. Whereas a **talisman** is constructed for the purpose of being imbued with powers from an incantation or spell for a particular purpose.

Long before the coming of Christ there were metal and stone workers in Scotland whose chief occupation was the manufacture of ornaments to ward off evil spirits. Eventually the makers of these magic artifacts began putting them into special settings and from the eighth to the twelfth centuries penannular (ring shaped) brooches of Celtic ore began to appear for magic purposes; baser metals were subsequently being replaced by gold and silver from the thirteenth to the sixteenth centuries.

Used as charms against disease and ill-luck these amulets, fashioned into brooches, were mostly circular with black engraved inlay. They first bore a variety of magic symbols, and then Latin tags like *O Mater Die* or *Memento mori*.

One brooch with power to cure the sick and protect the vulnerable was the famous brooch of Lorne, a silver disc with a massive socket capped with a huge crystal set inside a crenellated border. Round this were eight turrets each topped with a large pearl. Rumoured to have been a jewel lost by Robert I, the Bruce, at the battle of Dail Righ (Dalry) in Killin, Perth, in 1306, the brooch for many years belonged to the Bragheen Campbells, then became the property of the Macdougals of Dunollie for more than a century.

In Canto II of *Lord of the Isles*, Sir Walter Scott hinted at the brooch's mystic potency:

'Whence the brooch of burning gold
That clasps the Chieftain's mantle-fold,
Wrought and chased with rare device,
Studded fair with gems of price,
On the varied tartans beaming,
As, through night's pale rainbow gleaming,
Fainter now, now seen afar,
Fitful shines the northern star?

Gem! ne'er wrought on Highland mountain,
Did the fairy of the fountain,
Or the mermaid of the wave,
Frame three in some coral cave?
Did, in Iceland's darksome mine,
Dwarf's swat hands thy metal twine?
Or mortal-moulded, comest thou here,
From England's love, or France's fear?

To which Walter Scott added the footnote: 'A studded brooch, said to have been that which King Robert lost upon this occasion, was long preserved in the family of Macdougal, and was lost in a fire which consumed their temporary residence.'

Another brooch similar to that of Lorne was that of Lochbuie, said to have been made by a *cearden* (tinker) from silver found on Lochbuie estate on the Isle of Mull, Argyllshire. In 1855 this famous gem was acquired by the British Museum.

Large, bulbous and ring-shaped the mystic Skaill brooches (found in 1858 at Skaill, Orkney), have a mixed parentage. Said to have been struck at Baghdad in AD 945, they are curiously Viking Jellinge in style, and the monster designs are typical of Norse custom in amulet-making.

Perhaps the most popular mystic brooch in Scotland is the heart, or **Luckenbooth brooch**. They were made from around AD 1700 and their name comes from the luckenbooths (lock-up booths) set around the High Kirk of St Giles, Edinburgh, where the silversmiths carried on their business. In fact these brooches were made all over Scotland. Shaped like a heart these brooches would sometimes have a crown on the upper part and might be of two hearts intertwined. They were mostly given as love tokens when a couple became betrothed, but they were also used for magical purposes. Sometimes they were worn among the clothes on the left thigh to keep away witches' spells, and the story goes that nursing mothers wore them to stop witches drying up their milk, or indeed harming their infants. But from Banff to Balmerino they were used to avert the Evil Eye.

Scottish pearls come from a species of mussel which lives in rivers and these beautiful phenomena were long considered magic too. The Crown of Scotland is adorned with them for potency and many a craftsman used them on amulets to make people pure and chaste.

For centuries those who made amulets and talismans were either greatly venerated or mortally feared for their supposed powers. In Scotland in particular the use and manufacture of these charms became a capital crime. In 1678 Sir George Mackenzie of Rosehaugh, King's Advocate, tried to justify the barbarity:

'Though charms be not able to produce the effects that are punishable in witches, yet since these effects cannot be produced without the devil, and [since] he will not employ himself at the desire of any who have not resigned themselves wholly to him, it is very just that the users of these should be punished, being guilty at least of apostasy and heresy.'

Coins have long been used for jewellery too and in time such items became revered for their good luck qualities, particularly the emotive '**touch pieces**'. 'Touch pieces' were minted and distributed in England at 'healing by touch' ceremonies, especially for scrofula (King's Evil), a disease marked by chronic swellings of the glands in various parts of the body, particularly the neck, which tended to suppurate. Edward the Confessor is the first English King on record, in AD 1058, to 'touch' for scrofula, and he became a popular saint in medieval Scotland (Balmerino Abbey, Fife, was dedicated to him).

Both Tudor and Stuart monarchs utilised the 'gold angel' in touching, the coin symbolically showing St Michael the Archangel's defeat of the Devil. Many of these coins were punched for suspension around the neck or over a diseased member. Charles II medalets bore the inscription *Soli deo gloria* (To God alone be the Glory) and his nephew James Edward Stuart, the Old Pretender, claimed regal healing powers too, as did Charles Edward Stuart and Henry Stuart, his sons. When James Edward Stuart visited Glamis Castle in AD 1716 he 'touched' for the King's Evil in the castle chapel, and it was said 'all the patients recovered'. Coins given out by the pretender James VIII and III on that occasion were invested with magic potency.

So all classes of Scots invested jewels with magic power and the centre-stones of each piece were given significance if the stones were chosen to match the wearer's month of birth according to this system:

Garnet (red, sometimes brown, green, yellow and black; green was considered an unlucky colour for all not born in May; brown stood for fading affection), *January*, for truth and constancy.

Amethyst (bluish-violet, a grave colour but useful in restoring health to the sick), *February*, denoted sincerity, and helped to keep the wearer sober.

Bloodstone (dark green variegates with red jasper), *March*, for courage and presence of mind.

Diamond, *April*, for innocence and light.

Emerald, *May*, for love potency.

Pearl or *Agate*, *June*, the latter representing health and long life and a counter against poison, while the pearl stood for tears as well.

Ruby (Cornelian), *July*, contentment, courage.

Sardonyx (reddish), *August*, for married bliss.

Sapphire, *September*, the magic stone of Jupiter, an antidote for misery.

Opal, *October*, stood for hope, but unlucky for those not born in this month.

Topaz, *November*, fidelity.

Turquoise, *December*, prosperity.

Enchanted Places

THE veneration of certain locations in Scotland, from prehistoric standing stone sites to islands set in lochs, lasted in superstitious potency up to medieval times and much later. According to the records of the Presbytery of Elgin for 1649 one Andro Man was accused of idolatry by setting up a stone pillar and capering before it in some superstitious rite. The stone was broken up by the order of the Presbytery.

Yet, for a thousand years folk would gather all over Scotland at dolmens and menhirs to say prayers to the old spirits of the place, or ask blessings or cures. For instance, the ancient chambered tomb of **Carraig an Talaidh** ('stone of the lulling'), in Argyll, was long known as the 'Toothie Stone' for its efficacy in curing toothache. What you had to do was drive a nail into the stone at midnight to rid yourself of what Robert Burns called 'thou hell o a' diseases'.

Many an ancient hilltop fort has been invested in the superstitious tales of giants, who were deemed to have built them in the arcane past. And from Old Deer, Aberdeenshire, to the Dwarfie Stone, in Orkney, curious barrows and rock indentations are pointed out as the tombs of such creatures. Another such is **Edin's Hall Broch**, the supposed home of a three-headed giant called Etin. In reality it is an Iron Age dwelling on the north-east slope of Cockburn Law, Berwickshire, but in local superstition it was a dreadful place to visit for fear that the giant would 'slice the heart of the unwary for this supper'; thus the place was shunned.

When invaders hit Scotland's glens and hills, people buried their valuables, and traditions arose of hidden treasure all over Scotland. And to keep people away from possible sites, treasure hunters invented ghostly protectors and dragon guardians. And what better guardian to terrify the superstitious than the dragon. This warlike emblem, the symbol of Christian hell, had been the device the Viking raiders of

Scotland had carried on their shields; and the prows of their ships had been carved into the heads of dragons. And wherever King Arthur was mentioned in Scotland, from Dumbarton Rock to Eildon Hill, his store of arms and booty was protected by the golden dragon which Arthur's father, Uther Pendragon, had borne upon his royal standard.

Beginning in the Far North these were places deemed enchanted:

SHETLAND

Greflabbas Knowe, Sandsting, is where you could see ancient Picts dancing at certain times, the superstitious said. *Fear Breagach* ('counterfeit men') the single stones were called, for once two people had been turned to stone here for watching the ghostly Picts.

Haltadans, Fetlar, the stones and circle of the 'limping dance', was the haunt of *trows*, those curious dwarflike creatures who danced to fiddle music. Once a group of *trows* danced till the sun came up, and as punishment the spirits of the place turned them and their fiddlers (the nearby cairns) into stone. At Haltadans cures for disabled limbs and war wounds could be sought.

Harold's Cave, Unst, is the supposed resting place of King Harold of Norway and contains a rich treasure, the old folk said. But it is protected by an 'evil creature' who moves it underground to a different location should you try to dig for it.

Trows can be very mischievous and malevolent creatures, but you are safe from them as long as they do not materialise, the old saws commented. So if you walk alone at midnight around the **Rounds of Tivla, Unst**, you will be able to keep the *trows* from making their presence known in your vicinity for all time. The 'rounds' are three round cairns, with retaining circles.

Dragons and moving stones may be encountered at:

ORKNEY

Maes Howe, Stenness, forms one of the finest chamber tombs in Europe and the old chronicles tell us that it is the dwelling of Haugbui, who takes his name from the old Norse for ghost. The tomb is protected by a dragon inscribed on the site, and its four clawed feet, curious tail and fish-like head are pure Viking and fit nicely into the local stories of the monsters who lived in the sea hereabouts and harried the fishermen of old.

The Stone of Quoybune, Birsay moves about every Hogmanay as the Orkney clocks strike midnight. It moves slowly from its site to the Loch of Boardhouse, makes obeisance to the spirits of the water, dips itself therein and returns to its usual resting place. The local superstition still recalls how unlucky it is to observe this mystic perambulation; many a person has been found stone dead, or incapacitated beside the stone on New Year's Day for daring to peek.

THE OUTER HEBRIDES

The stones of **Callanish**, Uig, Lewis, the wise ones said, could not be counted for they were never the same twice running at the cruciform site. Many thought that these megaliths were actually giants which had been turned to stone by St Kiaran, and, up to 1814, the local schoolmaster Magnus Spence reported, at Beltane (1 May, the Celtic feast when the cattle were taken to summer pastures) and Midsummer, people gathered at the stones to light fires and perform 'certain immemorial rites'. Once it was the custom for young couples to plight their troth at the stones, and several actually consummated their union within the ancient circles to unlock the fertility potency of the stones.

Sanctuary Stone, North Uist. The superstition that sanctuary at sacred places was an inalienable right of all, even miscreants, began in early times when fugitives were granted refuge in churches and churchyards. The Celts would place those deemed guilty in the care of the priests of their cults until a proper trial could be secured, and all over Scotland the relics of the sanctuary boundaries are to be seen. Here at North Uist, on the *Cnoc mhic Eoghainn* ('the mound of Ewan's son') stands the sanctuary stone that protected many an accused. Incidentally in more Christian times the rights of sanctuary passed to the gyrth crosses which were set up in villages from that at Dull, Perthshire, to the Stob Cross stone at Balbirnie, near Markinch, Fife.

SKYE AND ROSS AND CROMARTY

The Trumpan Churchyard Stone, Vatternish, named 'the Heaven stone', reflects in Christian terms what the superstitious Norsemen thought about their afterlife in Valhalla, the great hall of the palace of Gladsheim in Asgard, wherein gathered the spirits of the brave dead. It was the Norse custom for those wishing to note the outcome of an event in terms of success to place their hand through or in the hole in a sacred stone. If the hand was placed (with the eyes shut) directly through the hole – without touching the sides – then a successful outcome would be anticipated; the reverse followed if the flesh touched the sides. When christianised the Vatternish stones indicated whether or not the petitioner would go to Heaven or Hell following the same ritual.

At **Applecross**, Ross and Cromarty, the locals varied the Vatternish ritual by putting their heads into the holed stones within the Applecross stone circle. In 1656 the Presbyter of Dingwall condemned the practice of people trying to find out the omens of forthcoming journeys in this way. But for two centuries after this the folk of Ross and Cromarty continued to come to Applecross to seek for signs and portents.

At **Gairloch**, Ross and Cromarty, the Celts were often referred to as the 'long-haired ones' (*gruagaich*) by later inhabitants, so at the stone called *clach na Gruagaich* the spirits of the Celtic dead were petitioned. As time went by the superstitious identified these spirits as Brownies, and left offerings for these creatures in the hollows of the stones. The most potent offering, of course, was milk which was thought to encourage the Brownies mystically to protect the neighbouring cattle.

SUTHERLAND

Plightin' Stane o'Lairg. Once this stone was built into a wall belonging to the glebe of the old parish church of Lairg. It was a celebrated meeting place for those wishing to seal a bargain, pledge faith, or swear an oath, including the pledging of romantic troth. The superstitious averred that such a transaction agreed while touching the stone, the bargain could not be cancelled or broken by witchcraft or the wishes of evildoers. In the mid-nineteenth century the church was pulled down and the stone removed; later the stone was donated to the Archaeological Museum, Toronto, Canada, where it is still exhibited.

FIFE

Fife offers a number of treasure sites, recount the old tales, from the gold mines set in the slopes of the Lomonds to the 'kist [chest] o' gold' at **Tower Hill**, Tayport. On the slopes of the hill a balladeer sat and wrote this:

'Here I sit and here I see
St Andrews, Broughty and Dundee,
And as mickle below as would buy all three
In a kist.'

But the biggest treasure of all was said to lie on **Norrie's Law**, Largo, where the Bronze Age barrow – named after a cowherd Tammie Norrie of Balmain – was long cited by the old folk as a location of vast riches. And the superstitious were right, for the area yielded Pictish silverware in 1819 and 1839. And perhaps there's more, for the superstitious used to say that there was so much gold hereabouts that when sheep lie down, their fleece turns the yellow of gold.

TAYSIDE

In Tayside, too, are the hill forts known as the **White** and **Brown Caterthun**, Menmuir, which the superstitious said had been built by witches as a fairy stronghold. At the White Caterthun is a large stone by the north rampart which is said to have been dropped in error by one of the witch builders; anyone touching the stone, when it is bathed by moonlight, would come into a considerable legacy. Sir Walter Scott was fascinated by the story and visited the Caterthun which inspired

85

him to write a poem in 1796 which include these lines
hinting at the superstition:

'Or if we trust the Village tale
A wayward maid in witching hour
When the stars were red and moon was pale
Rear'd thy dread mound by magic power.'

Guinevere's burial mound, Meigle, Angus. Burial
grounds have always been deemed magic places and
none more so than those linked with folk heroes and
heroines. Medieval legend linked King Arthur with the
somnolent village of Meigle, Perthshire, in such a way
as to make its churchyard enchanted land. Arthur's wife,
the beautiful Guinevere, known in Scotland as Vanona,
was captured, the medieval chroniclers say, by the court
rebel Sir Mordred, who imprisoned her at his castle of
Barry Hill, near Alyth.

Somewhat unfaithful, Guinevere, who already had
had dalliance with Sir Lancelot of the lake, now
fell for the charms of Sir Mordred. Needless to say
the long-suffering Arthur was put out, and besieged
Mordred's Perthshire fortress and, capturing it, ordered
that Guinevere be put to death by being buried at Meigle
in a mound still to be seen in the churchyard. The local
superstitious recorded that no pregnant woman should
walk on, stamp on, or sit down on the mound for fear of
miscarriage. Many, too, associated one of the 25 sculp-
tured monuments at Meigle museum to the Guinevere
legend, pointing out that one of the largest had covered
Guinevere's grave to make sure that her faithless soul did
not wander. In truth the Meigle stones pre-date Arthurian
times, but superstition was never thwarted by historical
dates!

In writing his play *Mary Rose*, Sir James Matthew
Barrie was thinking of the old Scots superstitions
regarding **islands** when he plotted the story which
told how a young mother mysteriously disappears on
an island in the Outer Hebrides, leaving her infant son
behind. The woman returns to her home 20 years later,
unchanged by time, and finds her son a grown man. The
island which inspired Barrie was in the middle of Loch

Voshimid, Outer Hebrides, which the author identified as 'the island that liked to be visited'. Barrie explained to his friends the old legends that people had been known to vanish on such islands, and years went by in which the vanished ones did not grow any older; and on their return to the mortal world they found their friends had died or had greatly aged.

The superstition that islands could 'kidnap' people is an old one in Scotland, thus the old folk who so believed were not in the least surprised by the newspaper reports on the disappearance of lighthouse keepers in the **Flannan Isles**, bynamed the Seven Hunters, set out in the North Atlantic, some 20 miles off Gallan Head, Lewis, in the Outer Hebrides. The year was 1900 and the relief ship *Hesperus* made her way slowly through the bad weather to relieve the lighthouse on Eilean Mor. When the *Hesperus* took up her anchorage position there was no sign of James Ducat, the chief keeper, nor his assistants Thomas Marshall and Donald Mortimer.

Although the keepers had vanished all seemed to be well, and a full-scale investigation never discovered where the lighthouse keepers had gone, or why they seemed to have left their posts without trace. The official statement of the Northern Lighthouse Board said, 'It must be concluded that the three men had left their posts possibly to secure gear and to ascertain the exact extent of storm damage at the landing stage, and were there caught by an unexpectedly heavy sea and drowned.'

No experienced lighthouse keeper really accepted this statement and averred that no knowledgeable keepers would all have ventured out in bad weather to the perilous spots on Eilean Mor. Many believed that the island itself had spirited the keepers away, and the superstitious reported that most of the small islands in Scottish water had 'voices' of their own that lured sailors to their death. They also said that the ghostly voices of drowned fishermen can be heard off the islands' coasts crying for help.

The story inspired the poet Wilfred Wilson Gibson to write this about the incident:

'Aye, though we hunted high and low, and hunted
   everywhere
Of the three men's fate we found no trace,
Of any kind in any place
But a door ajar, and an untouch'd meal
And on·overtopped chair;
And as we listened in the gloom of that forsaken
   livingroom,
A chill clutch on our breath,
We thought how ill-chance came to all who kept
   the Flannan Light . . .
And long we thought of the three we sought —
And of what might yet befall.'

Islands large and small were long considered prime
places for the carrying out of magic ritual, undoubtedly
a race memory of the 'sacred groves' of the Druids who
chose islands for their secret rites within a silvan setting.
One such island was Eilean Maree on **Loch Maree**,
Ross and Cromarty. Here mysterious rites in the name
of St Maebrubhan were enacted as a 'christianisation'
of the rituals of the Celtic god Mourie, whose devotees
pointed out his sacred well and tree, and offered votive
libations of milk in his honour. So in time of plague or
war, or need for a community to petition the spirits of
earth and air for protection against evil, superstitious
Scots swam or rowed out to the thousands of islands
in sea and loch to seek answers to their problems.